WHEELS
DOWN

WHEELS DOWN

ADJUSTING TO LIFE AFTER DEPLOYMENT

BRET A. MOORE AND **CARRIE H. KENNEDY**

Published by
APA Lifetools
750 First Street, NE
Washington, DC 20002
www.apa.org

To order
APA Order Department
P.O. Box 92984
Washington, DC 20090-2984
(800) 374-2721; (202) 336-5510
Fax: (202) 336-5502
TDD/TTY: (202) 336-6123
Online: www.apa.org/pubs/books/
E-mail: order@apa.org

In the U.K., Europe, Africa, and the Middle East, copies may be ordered from
American Psychological Association
3 Henrietta Street
Covent Garden, London
WC2E 8LU England

Typeset in Sabon by Circle Graphics, Columbia, MD

Printer: United Book Press, Inc., Baltimore, MD
Cover Designer: Naylor Design, Washington, DC

The opinions and statements published are the responsibility of the authors, and such opinions and statements do not necessarily represent the policies of the American Psychological Association.

The views expressed in this book are those of the authors and do not reflect the official policy or position of the Department of the Army, Department of the Navy, Department of Defense, or the United States Government.

Library of Congress Cataloging-in-Publication Data
Moore, Bret A.
  Wheels down : adjusting to life after deployment / Bret A. Moore and Carrie H. Kennedy.
    p. cm.
  Includes bibliographical references and index.
  ISBN-13: 978-1-4338-0872-2
  ISBN-10: 1-4338-0872-2
  ISBN-13: 978-1-4338-0873-9 (e-book)
  ISBN-10: 1-4338-0873-0 (e-book)
  1. Veterans—Mental health—United States. 2. Deployment (Strategy)—Social aspects—United States. 3. Post-traumatic stress disorder. 4. Combat—Psychological aspects. I. Kennedy, Carrie H. II. Title.

  UH629.3.M665 2011
  355.1'29—dc22
                                    2010012949

British Library Cataloguing-in-Publication Data
A CIP record is available from the British Library.

Printed in the United States of America
First Edition

To all the selfless men and women in uniform
serving around the world.

CONTENTS

Contents

PREFACE

At the time this book was written, nearly two million service members had deployed since the attacks on the World Trade Center. If you are reading this book, you are likely one of those two million. Many of you have served multiple tours in multiple locations, logging anywhere from a few months to a few years in hostile and austere environments.

As an informed service member, you know that you can read any newspaper or watch the news any day and see reports about the war and a multitude of concerns about the physical and mental health of service members. Sometimes these news reports are right, sometimes they are partially right, and other times they are nothing more than sensational stories created to sell papers or fill airtime. But they can leave questions in the minds of service members. Am I all right? Do I have a stress disorder? Has deployment changed me? Why am I chronically ticked off? Why am I not getting along the same with my spouse? Do I have permanent brain damage from a brain injury? The questions go on.

The stress of being separated from family and friends, reliving the same day over and over again (what some call the *Groundhog Day phenomenon*), and the fear and uncertainty of combat have an impact on every service member. It is important that you understand what that impact might be and that you have the information you need to have. For this reason, we wrote this book primarily for the service member who has returned from deployment, although we also provide some advice for deployment situations because we assume that many of you will deploy again.

Although much of our advice is geared toward veterans of Operations Iraqi and Enduring Freedom, most of the information in this book is also for those returning from ships and deployments to places such as Korea, Japan, Italy, Germany, and Guantanamo Bay.

It is important for you to know that we have a tremendous amount of respect for what you do. We know how difficult deployment can be and that adjusting to being back home is filled with many challenges and obstacles. Always remember that your job is one that the average citizen cannot understand. You are a protector of our nation. So, before you start reading this book, we ask that you take a minute and reflect on where you have been and what you have accomplished. We're sure you have heard the expression "freedom isn't free." And that's true. People die in war, and people come back changed from deployment. Your job is one of the hardest and most important jobs in the nation. If we have done *our* job, this book will help you with some of the rougher parts of *your* job so that you can stay in peak mental shape for yourself, your family, and the military. Godspeed!

ACKNOWLEDGMENTS

Without the support of many people in our lives, this book would have not been possible. We would like to thank our families for their encouragement and patience. We are grateful for the professionalism and dedication of the publishing staff in the Books department at the American Psychological Association, specifically Maureen Adams and Daniel Brachtesende. Finally, we would like to thank our mentors, both civilian and military.

WHEELS DOWN

INTRODUCTION

There's a lot of news coverage out there about service members coming back from deployment all messed up. If you read or hear too much of it, you might become convinced that not only do you all have "issues," but that these problems are destined to last for the rest of your lives. It is true that every service member has to make an adjustment from a war zone or other deployment to being back home again, but unfortunately much of the coverage seen in the media has more to do with sensationalism and less to do with facts.

Much of what service members experience after returning from deployment is actually quite normal. You can randomly choose any person off the street, drop him or her in Afghanistan for 12 months, and feel confident that he or she will have a difficult time on returning home. However, you have something that separates you from the average citizen. You have training . . . and a lot of it.

Training is probably the most protective factor for you when it comes to meeting challenges while deployed. You have been taught how to react in stressful and dangerous situations, but you have also been trained in how to stay focused on your job and not get sidetracked by annoyances that can put you or others at risk. You've been taught how to manage stress and how maintaining a predictable routine keeps you physically and mentally strong. These are just a few things that separate you from the average Joe or Jane. With that being said, we realize that sometimes training is not enough. Some of you will have a more difficult time than others after returning from deployment, and face it, some things happen that you just can't prepare for. When something isn't quite right, you should be able to recognize what the problem is and know what to do about it. And you'll be glad to know that this doesn't usually mean that you need to see a shrink.

Throughout this book, we provide you with basic guidance and advice on how to manage some of the more common problems service members report after returning from deployment. However, before we go any further, it's important to define what *postdeployment* refers to. *Postdeployment* simply refers to the process of returning home after deployment, which is also often referred to as *redeployment*. For the National Guard or Reserve, this could mean returning home to your civilian job and family after your commitment is up. For active-duty service members, this refers to returning to your permanent duty station or to civilian life if you have decided to leave the military.

The chapters in this book are based on some of the more common issues we have seen service members deal with postdeployment. In Chapter 1, we provide you with an overview of what the first hours, days, and months will be like after you return home. Chapter 2 focuses on anger, a common problem that service members are forced to deal with, and we provide you with a number of tips on managing your anger. In Chapter 3, we address sleep or, more accurately, the lack of it and what you can do about it. Chapter 4 covers an issue that is all too often encountered when working with service members— financial problems. Whether you spent all your money while deployed or a loved one cleaned you out through a power of attorney, we discuss what things you can do to get back on track financially. Unfortunately, divorce and breakups are also relatively common occurrences during deployment, so in Chapter 5, we provide you with some tips on how to handle being single again. In Chapter 6, we discuss what to expect with your children. They have grown and changed while you were gone. This in itself is not a bad thing, but you may find that old ways of parenting may not be as effective as they used to be. Chapter 7 addresses how deployment is different for women. Chapter 8 helps you identify whether your drinking, drug use, or gambling has gotten out of control and what you can do about it if it has become a problem. In Chapter 9, we teach you about grief related to the death of a friend or fellow service member. Chapter 10 covers the psychological, moral, and spiritual aspects of taking another human's life during combat. Chapter 11 deals with hyperstartle, or the exaggerated startle response, and Chapter 12 covers the symptoms of and treatment for posttraumatic stress disorder. In Chapter 13, we discuss the concept of mild traumatic brain injury and what you can expect if you suffered a concussion during your deployment. Chapter 14 addresses the very serious issue of suicide. Unfortunately, suicide has been on the rise in the military over the past several years. We provide you with some advice and guidance on how to address suicidal thinking in yourself and in others. Chapter 15 covers an emerging area of psychology that believes people can actually grow psychologically stronger after trauma. Yes, many people actually become stronger, happier, and more productive after challenging events. Last, we have included an Appendix that lists various resources for you and your family.

Keep in mind that you don't have to read this whole book to get what you need. Each chapter stands on its own, so if you have a specific concern, go straight to that chapter. However, we encourage you to read as many of the chapters as you can find time to with your busy schedule. It may turn out that more chapters than you thought can help you. Also, share this book with a friend once you're done reading it. It may help him or her as well.

Remember, everyone has an adjustment when they get back home. This book will help you better understand your own deployment experience and put it into perspective.

We should note that although we have tried to put everything we could think of to tell you in this book, it can't be a substitute for seeking professional help if you need it. We obviously can't re-create here some of the expertise you might need. Some of you are dealing with significant problems; if that is the case, your best course of action is to seek the services of a trained professional. This book will guide you and help you figure out whether you need help and where to get it.

CHAPTER 1

THE HOMECOMING

For many of you, preparing to come home from deployment is an exciting and hopeful time in your life. Your thoughts are likely consumed with being reunited with your family and friends, buying that new car you dreamed about with all the money you saved up, or simply savoring that first cheeseburger and beer at your favorite local bar or restaurant. It's a moment to think back to all the good times you had with your fellow service members and an opportunity to be thankful that you're about to be out of harm's way.

However, for others, preparing for the long trip home can involve much stress and anxiety. It's a safe bet to say that every person reading this book knows of a least one service member who has come back from a deployment to find a broken marriage, an unfaithful boyfriend or girlfriend, an empty bank account, or permanent change-of-station orders to the most remote and austere post, base, or billet that only the hardest of the hard could appreciate. Heck, maybe that person is you. Our ultimate point is that not all postdeployment periods are the same. They are as different as each and every one of you. For some, things are back to normal within a week or two. For others, it can take many months. Some people even prefer to return to the war zone because this has begun to feel normal, whereas life back in the States doesn't.

> **Quick Fact**
>
> Returning from a deployment can be both a joyous and a stressful process.

Most of you have probably heard one or two postdeployment horror stories. In one instance, a service member returned home to find his girlfriend married to another man. Apparently, she forgot to mention this during their phone conversations while the service member was deployed. After returning from a 12-month deployment, another service member was surprised to find that his Harley Davidson had been sold without his knowledge (be careful with those power of attorneys; see more about this in Chapter 4). Last, although this one is believed to be military folklore, there's the one about the mother using a power of attorney to reenlist her son without his knowledge while he was deployed, even though he wanted to leave the military.

There are a million and one postdeployment horror stories out there, and many of them tend to be exaggerated for entertainment value. However, postdeployment can be a difficult process, and it is likely that you will have some difficulty adjusting.

The goals for this chapter are twofold. First, we want you to know what to expect when you return home from a deployment. As you will learn throughout this book, perceptions and expectations shape much of your experiences. We want you to be prepared. Being knowledgeable about what the first few days, weeks, and months have in store for you will help you ease back into your old life. Second, we will provide you with some tips to help your transition go a little more smoothly. Remember, things will not be perfect. You will encounter hurdles, but nothing greater than those you have already dealt with.

BEFORE REDEPLOYMENT

If you are reading this before returning from deployment, you are likely experiencing a number of different emotions. One minute you may be excited, and the next you may be nervous. You may have periods of hopefulness, which may be countered by feelings of uncertainty. This is not uncommon. Depending on your particular situation, you've been thinking about returning home for 3, 6, 7, or 12 or more months. You think you know what to expect and how things will be when you get back, but you're not sure. On one hand, your expectations are high. You fantasize about holding your significant other on that first night back or spending some quality time with your children. You imagine how nice it will be to drive the open road on that new bike or in that new car waiting so patiently for you back home. But on the other hand, you also contemplate questions such as "Has my wife changed?" "Will my child recognize me?" or "How will I manage my finances when I'm making less money?" It's an emotional roller coaster, to say the least. The good news is that you can prepare your mind for this transition. Think about it. You wouldn't return home with your unit without completing a redeployment health assessment or an up-to-date sensitive items inventory. So, why wouldn't you have your mind squared away? Here are a few things that can help.

Be Realistic

You've been gone a while. Things have changed. If you set your expectations too high, you are more likely to be disappointed. For example, you may be expecting to have earth-shattering and record-breaking periods of sex with your significant other that first night back. Unfortunately, your partner may not be thinking the same thing, which sets the stage for disappointment and resentment right out of the gate. Keep in mind that you may not be on the same page

> ### Quick Fact
>
> It's important to take things slowly when you get back. Your spouse or significant other may need some time to feel comfortable again with intimacy.

as your partner on this subject. He or she may have some issues that need to be resolved first, or he or she simply may not have been able to find a babysitter. Furthermore, for some people, it takes time to rekindle the flame, and periods of courting and nonsexual intimacy (e.g., talking, holding hands, and, yes, cuddling) are required. Just talk with your partner about this issue.

Rehearse What You Want to Say and Do

The old saying "practice makes perfect" is sound advice. Before you get back home, practice in your head over and over what you plan to say to your loved ones or how you will handle difficult situations. For example, if you know that parents, siblings, friends, and the like will be expecting you to spend time with them those first few hours, but your wife, husband, children, and so forth are expecting the same, then have a script ready and rehearsed that will help you set boundaries and minimize hurt feelings.

Think About Ways in Which You Have Changed

It is very likely that you have changed during your deployment. Some changes may be good, and some may not be so good. Ask yourself, "How have I changed since I left home?" "Do I get frustrated more easily now?" "Are my life goals different than 6 months or a year ago?" or something along those lines. Having a better sense of who you are and where you see your life heading can help you communicate more effectively with your family, career officer, and fellow service members. As your military training has already taught you, understanding a problem and being able to communicate the solution effectively is 90% of the job.

THE FIRST FEW DAYS

The first few days home can be the most stressful. If your experience is like most, you will be shuttled back and forth so you can stand in more formations so that some military brass or other governmental official you don't know can thank you for your service. You will attend a series of briefings on subjects such as safe driving, safe drinking, and safe sex, and most likely view yet another PowerPoint presentation on psychological readjustment by someone like the authors of this book. Although this will likely annoy you, these things are all important, and we strongly encourage you to listen and follow the recommendations provided. Things will be hectic for those first 72 hours. In addition to being pulled in a dozen different directions, you will probably be suffering from jet lag, sleep deprivation, and extreme agitation because you are ready to be released from your unit so you can go be with your family. Take the case of SPC D., for example.

SPC D. landed at Ft. Hood, Texas, at 0100 hours after a 23-hour flight and 5 days spent "sleeping" in a tent in Kuwait waiting for that flight. As soon as he steps off the plane and breathes in the fresh Texas air, his first sergeant yells at him for holding up the line. After catching up with the rest of his unit, he stands in line for 2 hours waiting to swipe his ID card and another hour to turn his weapon into the armory. After taking a 30-minute bus ride to the post, he joins his unit in a formation where they stand for another 30 minutes while the final touches are put on the reception in the gymnasium. After the reception is over, he is able to spend a few minutes with his family who came to see him. His unit is finally dismissed but told to report to the parade field at 0630 hours for a second reception. He decides not to sleep. After spending several hours that morning at the parade field, his unit is shuttled back to the office to receive a few briefings and discuss the schedule for the next several days. Once dismissed, SPC D. rushes to the hotel where his family is staying. It's obvious that they are upset, and they complain to him that they drove more than 7 hours to see him, but he has barely been able to spend a few minutes with them. He feels that they are blaming him for things he has no control over. Upset, he goes out that evening with his friends and gets drunk. On the drive home, he is pulled over by the police and taken to jail for driving under the influence. He is also charged with possession of a concealed weapon because his personal firearm was under his seat. Here are a few things that could have made SPC D.'s transition go a little easier.

Remind Yourself That the Chaos and Drama Will Be Over Soon

"This too shall pass." We're not really sure where this old saying comes from, but it is certainly sound advice. Tell yourself over and over that things will start to settle down in a few days. Your superiors will relax once all the equipment is accounted for, and once your family and friends get that initial fix, they'll begin to place fewer demands and expectations on you. Plus, you will have had the opportunity to rest in a real bed, eat at one or two of your favorite restaurants, and become familiar with your favorite television shows again. It's only a matter of time before things start to feel normal again.

Get Plenty of Sleep

Sitting in tents and makeshift airport terminals, a long and noisy intercontinental flight, and the mound of responsibilities required of you during those first 12 hours make it nearly impossible to get a decent amount of real sleep. Our advice is to sleep as much as possible during the first few days back, even if it's only for a few hours. Listen to your body. If you are wide awake after 3 hours, then get up. If you are still sleepy after 8 hours, keep sleeping. Your internal clock is out of whack at this point, but it will reset itself. Remember, lack of sleep makes you grouchier and less able to concentrate, and it prevents you from handling things effectively.

Set Boundaries

As we mentioned earlier, many of your friends, family members, and general acquaintances are going to want to spend time with you when you get back. The problem is that there is only so much of you. So, set boundaries. Determine your priorities as far as spending time with people. Let the rest know that you will make time for them shortly. It's your time to readjust, and you can't fully do that while you are trying to meet everyone else's needs. Remember, you can't please everyone, so don't stress yourself out trying to.

Don't Drink Alcohol

We know that many of you will think we are nuts or unrealistic for saying this, but stay away from the booze for a few days. Your tolerance is not what it used to be! Those of you who could easily knock back six to eight beers in an evening may only be able to handle two or three. This may make you a cheaper date, but it also puts you at risk of stupid behavior and alcohol blackouts after only a couple of beers. Pace yourself. You will have plenty of time to go partying with your friends. Please don't end up in the emergency room for alcohol poisoning or in jail for drunk driving your first night back.

Let Someone Else Drive

This is directed to those of you who did most of the driving while deployed. You are used to owning the roads over there. Driving down the middle of the highway in the States is typically frowned on. You can't throw a water bottle at a car just because it's following too close to you. And for Pete's sake, don't bump somebody off the road just because they are going too slow. Road rage is a common problem for returning service members. Reports have shown that returning service members have an increase in speeding and reckless driving tickets in the initial months after redeployment. And again, don't get behind the wheel if you decide to drink.

Leave the Weapons at Home

You have gotten used to carrying a weapon with you at all times while on deployment. Many of you were required to have them locked and loaded while on mission. Resist the urge to carry a weapon in your vehicle or when going out with family or friends. Leave it at home. Also, never use a weapon, loaded or unloaded, to intimidate someone else during a fight. You may even want to have family or friends keep your weapons for you until things have settled back to normal.

THE FIRST 30 TO 60 DAYS

Congratulations! You've made it through the first few days of being back home. Now let's get through the next 30. For most of you, much of your life will have returned to normal. Some of you will take leave, move to a new duty station, or leave the military for good. Others' units will develop new training schedules and prepare for their next deployment. In other words, things will be busy. From a psychological standpoint, your sleep schedule should start to return to normal, and your mood should start to level off. We said *start*. It can take many months for a person to reset things. Here are a few things that can help keep you on track.

Acknowledge When Something Is Not Quite Right

You know yourself better than anyone else knows you. If after several weeks your sleep isn't getting better, you are getting into frequent arguments with your spouse or significant other, or you are losing your temper more often, tell someone. It doesn't have to be a shrink. You can talk to your chaplain, squad leader, platoon leader or first sergeant, chief, or a friend that you trust. Sometimes just talking about your situation with someone who understands or someone who is a good listener helps. For example, it may help to talk with a spouse or a sibling, even though he or she may not fully understand everything you faced during the deployment. For more serious problems, talk with someone like us, a mental health professional. If you are drinking more than usual, having nightmares, feeling depressed, or finding it difficult to let go of something that happened during the deployment, military psychologists, psychiatrists, and social workers can help.

Develop a Routine That Works for You

Except for "hydrate, keep it pointed downrange, and don't be late to formation," the next most frequently heard piece of advice in the

---

Quick Fact

If you find yourself drinking or fighting more, feeling depressed, or not being able to let go of disturbing events that happened to you during the deployment, seek professional help.

---

military is to maintain a routine. This is sound advice. Routines help you regain and maintain control of yourself and your environment. Develop a new exercise regimen. Pencil in a recurring date night. Just create some predictability.

Take a Few Long Weekends

Use some of the leave you banked while you were deployed, and take a few 3- or 4-day weekends. Go on a road trip. Visit family or friends who live out of town. Turn off your cell phone and stay in bed. Watch movies on the couch with your significant other. Forget about work, the military, and the deployment.

Drink in Moderation

Yes, we have already talked about alcohol use. Just say no for the first few days. However, because alcohol use is part of the military culture and, frankly, it can make for a pretty fun night, we know that many of you will hit the clubs and bars pretty hard during those first several weeks. All we ask is that you drink in moderation. Take it slow. Pace yourself. Give your body a chance to adjust to the cheap beer and liquor served in the bars outside the post or base. And always have a designated driver and someone who will give you feedback when you've had too many.

Take a Look at Military OneSource

Miltary OneSource is one of the best military-friendly organizations out there. In addition to providing referrals for counseling by civilian mental health professionals, they provide assistance with financial planning, parenting education, deployment assistance, and many other useful benefits for service members. You can find them at http://www.militaryonesource.com. Check out the Appendix at the end of the book for information on this resource and others.

A FEW FINAL THOUGHTS

Most of you will soon be set in your routine, and life will return to an acceptable level of normalcy. Your relationships will be moving forward, and your military career (or civilian career, if you left the military) will be productive and rewarding. If you feel like you are on track, that's awesome. However, if you don't, keep in mind that it can take a while to adjust to being back home, especially if you have deployed more than once, something unusually awful happened on a deployment, or something unexpected was waiting for you back home. If a month or more has passed, however, and things aren't starting to look up, ask for help. We know you are tough and like to take care of yourself, but you have one of the toughest jobs in this country. Being a soldier, sailor, coast guardsman, airman, or marine is not a 9-to-5 job. It can be extremely stressful, and it can take a toll on you and your family. There is help out there, but if you don't ask for it, nobody can help you. Also, pay attention to your family. For most people, families are the single most stable source of support. Often, however, we take them for granted. Don't do that. Last, develop an identity outside of the military. You don't have to make the military less of a priority, just find something that defines you in addition to the U.S. Army, Coast Guard, Navy, Air Force, or Marine Corps. Maybe it's being a father, mother, community volunteer, spiritual leader, or baseball coach. Just diversify your identity.

CHAPTER 2

ANGER: HOW CAN IT BE HEALTHY AND KILL ME AT THE SAME TIME?

Do you find yourself getting upset at every little annoyance that comes your way? Do most of your conversations revolve around how stupid other people are or how unfair life is? Is your spouse complaining about your temper? Have you noticed that people don't seem to want to hang around you anymore? Or, to steal from the self-help genre, are you sweating the small stuff? If you can answer yes to any of these questions, then you are likely experiencing too much anger.

Anger is a very powerful emotion that often bothers service members after deployment. It can negatively affect your relationships with your friends and significant other, hurt your chances for promotion, increase your chances of getting sick, and cause you to pick a fight with someone twice your size at the local bar. But anger isn't all bad. Research has shown us that if anger is expressed in a controlled and socially acceptable manner, it can be quite beneficial. Specifically, it can promote productivity, effective communication, and sound mental health. Therefore, you don't need to be a person who never gets angry, you just need to learn how to control anger.

We are not looking to convince you to face your evil anger demons or embrace your inner angry child. We just want you to

> **Quick Fact**
>
> Excessive anger is a very common problem that service members deal with after deployment.

keep things in perspective. After all, you are soldiers, sailors, coast guardsmen, airmen, and marines. You are expected to be a little rough around the edges. If you are having problems with anger, however, it's important that you develop a balance so that you can be both a hard-charger in the field and a composed and respectful person on the street. What happens after deployment is that people sometimes forget how to manage the normal but sometimes difficult situations, events, and people in their lives. Being gone for 6 or 12 months can do this to a person. Add into the mix some of the things you may have experienced on deployment, and the transition from war zone to home life can be very agitating. Maybe you lost friends on the battlefield, were put into situations where you had to make impossible choices, did something you regret, have been left by your spouse or significant other, were passed over for promotion, or suffered abuses by an unfit leader. If you think about it, there are all kinds of things to be angry about.

With this being said, our main goals for this chapter are simple. First off, we want you to understand where anger comes from. In other words, how do you create it for yourself? (Make no mistake— you create *all* of your own emotions.) Second, we want you to understand that anger can be both harmful and helpful. Finally, we will provide you with some tips and techniques that will help you manage your anger and prevent you from making your life anymore difficult than it already is. In other words, follow this advice, and you won't do something stupid just because you're ticked off.

WHAT IS ANGER AND WHAT CAUSES IT?

Anger is often caused by having an unrealistic view of a situation, a lack of flexibility in problem solving, and all-or-nothing ways of thinking. Think back to the last time you got mad. What were you really mad about? Let's look at an example. Say CPL A. comes home from a hard day's work and is looking forward to hanging out with his girlfriend. This is what they do every Friday night, so why would this Friday be any different? He opens the door and finds her standing in front of the mirror dressed in her nicest red dress and putting on the finishing touches of her make-up. He asks, "Are you going somewhere? She says, "Yes, to the club with my girlfriends"—and he loses it. He makes comments such as "We always spend Friday night together," "You never want to spend time with me anymore," or "You'd rather be with some other guy than me." So, what's up with CPL A.? It's likely not that he is mad that his girlfriend has decided to spend time with her friends or that they have broken away from their Friday night tradition, but rather that he is afraid that she no longer loves him or that she is interested in finding someone better at the club. So, in this case, his anger is a direct result of his fear of losing her.

CPL A.'s anger is fueled by how he is looking at the situation. As we note frequently throughout this book, how you think about a situation and what you say to yourself about that situation determine how you feel about it. In this case, CPL A. views his girlfriend's desire to spend time with her friends as evidence that she no longer loves him and that she is looking for greener pastures. If you asked CPL A. what he was telling himself, you'd likely find that he was making comments to himself such as "She doesn't love me" or "She's going to meet another guy." Obviously, self-talk like this (we all talk to ourselves—we just don't do it out loud) is going to increase his unrealistic fears and only fuel his anger. Assuming that he has no evidence to support this, his views will only strain the relationship and possibly unintentionally push her away. Unrealistic views often

---

> **Quick Fact**
>
> Anger often comes from unrealistic and overblown views of situations.

---

drive anger, and anger is fueled by how we think about things. It is actually that simple.

THE MULTIPLE PERSONALITIES OF ANGER

Before we talk about tips and techniques to help you manage anger, we want to briefly discuss how anger can be both bad and good for you. If you have an understanding of how anger can create problems for you, then you will be more likely to do something about it. Also, when you are able to appreciate how anger can benefit you, then you will be able to maximize and harness it.

How Anger Can Hurt You

The negative impact of uncontrolled anger can be viewed in terms of social, interpersonal, and physical consequences. The negative social consequences of anger are those that will get you thrown in jail. Common examples after deployment include getting into a fight at the bar because someone from a different unit looked at you crossly or throwing an empty Gatorade bottle at another car on the highway because it cut you off.

Negative interpersonal consequences are those things you do that get you kicked out of your house and stuck on your friend's couch for a week, or keep you from getting invited to next year's Thanksgiving dinner. Anger that is not kept in check will almost certainly put a tremendous strain on your relationships with your

Quick Fact

Anger can lead to headaches, stomach problems, high blood pressure, and even death.

spouse or significant other, family, friends, and the people you work with. People can only handle so much complaining, bickering, and poor attitude before they start asking the question "Is it worth it?" Once you head down this road, it can be tough to get back on track.

The last area that excessive anger can negatively affect is your physical health. You don't need to be a doctor to know that anger causes stress and tension. Research in medicine and psychology has shown that stress and tension lead to headaches, stomach pain, insomnia, depression, anxiety, and high blood pressure. In extreme and chronic cases, uncontrolled anger can lead to a heart attack or stroke. Extreme anger can kill you. It can also lead to increased alcohol and tobacco use, which creates other problems.

How Anger Can Help You

Up to this point, it may seem like anger has gotten a bad rap. So, let's try and level the playing field a little. Anger can benefit you in a number of ways. For example, anger can help motivate you to make changes in your life. Think back to basic training or boot camp when you were struggling with some aspect of your physical, educational, or military training. It's quite possible that anger at your drill sergeant or drill instructor motivated you to run faster or do more push-ups, spend an extra hour at night studying for an exam, or practice the steps of breaking down and reassembling an assault rifle in your head before you passed out from fatigue on your cot. In these situations, anger motivated you to perform at your highest level.

Anger is also a very effective way of helping you learn to be more assertive in your interactions with others. Assertive communication is a nonaggressive way of letting people know how you feel, what your needs are, and what you expect of them. Actually, assertive communication is expected of you in the military. Unfortunately, many people do not learn this skill and either just come off looking angry and hostile or let others walk over them.

Turning anger into assertiveness is not that difficult. The first step is to acknowledge that you are angry. As with acknowledging any problem, this can be the hardest part. Second, take a few minutes to let the intensity of the emotion decrease. So CPL A. needs to take a step back so that he doesn't keep picking a fight with his girlfriend, making the situation worse. Third, determine what it is that you really want to say. What CPL A. wants to say is that he is disappointed that his girlfriend made other plans and that he was looking forward to spending time with her. Fourth, practice what you want to say. If CPL A. had followed the preceding steps rather than yelling at his girlfriend and throwing accusations at her, he could have expressed what he was really feeling: that he cares about her and wants to spend time with her. The final step is to say what you want to say. In CPL A.'s case, if he used assertive communication, a number of positive things could result. His girlfriend might change her plans or meet up with him later. Although she may not be able to cancel with her friends that night, she will be less likely in the future to make other plans on Friday nights. Both of them are likely to communicate better so that these kinds of misunderstandings about what their plans are don't happen again.

GETTING CONTROL OF YOURSELF

Controlling your anger is not as difficult and complicated as one may think. In the past, experts would tell you to just let it rip or vent until your heart is content. We have backed off a little on this one because all letting it rip seems to do is make things worse. Here are a few constructive things you can do.

Ask Yourself, "What Am I Really Angry About?"

Often people get angry over seemingly small things. Miscommunication is also the cause of unnecessary anger. Take a step back, analyze the situation, and decide whether the issue is worth getting angry about. Chances are, it isn't.

Change the Way You Think

Remember CPL A.? His problem was that he said a lot of negative things to himself and jumped to conclusions. Make sure to look for the evidence that supports your thoughts. You may be surprised to find that you jump to a lot of conclusions, just like CPL A. did. Instead of saying, "She must be going out to meet some other guy," try saying, "She just wants to spend time with her friends."

Leave

If you find that your anger is about to reach its peak, go somewhere else. Walk to a friend's house, visit a relative, or go get something to eat. In most cases, taking a little break will allow you the time to regroup and handle the situation better.

Take a Deep Breath

Relaxation is a great way to control your anger. Plus, it is very simple. All you need to do is close your eyes, take several deep breaths, and feel your body become less tense. You can also quietly repeat a calming word or phrase such as *relax* or the ever-popular *serenity now.*

If you do this for 10 minutes, your anger is practically guaranteed to decrease or even go away, and you will be more likely to think realistically about whatever the situation is.

Use Your Imagination

Closing your eyes and visualizing (pretending) you are at the beach, at a ball game, or some other place or event that makes you feel relaxed and calm is very effective (yes—two shrinks are actually telling you to go to your happy place). Let's say that 5 years ago you went to the beach with your significant other and spent the whole day soaking up the rays and listening to music. Obviously, this was a very peaceful and enjoyable time. Well, you can trick your mind into believing that you are at that place again even though it's 5 years later. Your mind doesn't know. It thinks you are there again. Consequently, it tells your body to relax, and you will start to notice that you are feeling those same emotions of happiness, joy, and contentment.

Take It Out on the Bag

If you get angry a lot, buying a punching bag is a great investment. If you don't have the money, work some of that anger off at the gym. Remember, free gym membership is one of the benefits of being in the military.

Laugh at Yourself

Learning to laugh at yourself when you overreact and blow a fuse can be very therapeutic. People tend to take things way too seriously. Ask yourself, "Is anyone going to care about this in 10 years?" or

"Is the world going to end because of this?" If not, take a step back and find the humor in the situation.

Avoid Situations That Make You Angry

This is the easiest one of all. If you know something or someone makes you angry, try and stay away from that something or someone at least until your postdeployment irritability starts wearing off. If it's something or someone you can't stay away from, then try the next technique.

Problem Solve

The military has taught you how to solve problems. Use your problem-solving abilities to control your anger. Although your branch of the service may have taught you a different method of problem solving, the standard approach is (a) define the problem, (b) generate possible solutions, (c) evaluate potential solutions, and (d) implement the preferred solution. For example, if you and your spouse fight every time you sit down to go over the monthly bills, figure out what has been causing the strife and try something different. If what you have been doing is not working, try something else, such as bringing in a neutral third party, such as a financial planner (see the Appendix) to help you both gain perspective. Or you can decide to deal with stressful situations only on the weekend when you and your spouse don't also have to deal with work pressures.

Seek Counseling

If all else fails, seek help from a professional. This can be your unit chaplain, your local pastor, or a base–post counselor or psychologist.

Please note that we recommend a number of times in this book that a chaplain is a good resource for you. Keep in mind that military chaplains are there for everyone, no matter what their religious beliefs. If you are an atheist, the chaplain is still a confidential person for you to talk to, and many people with a variety of religious beliefs have been helped by military chaplains. If you have a good chaplain and feel comfortable talking to that person, go for it. He or she isn't trying to convert you.

A FEW FINAL THOUGHTS

Controlling your anger is not an impossible task. It just takes some time, willingness to change, and a little effort. Uncontrolled anger has hurt entirely too many service members. If you are able to recognize that you have an anger problem and make the necessary corrections, you will lead a much more enjoyable and rewarding life. You have made it home. Don't spend your time fighting with your loved ones or wasting your time hating everything about life. Now is the time to be grateful for what you have and hopeful for what life will bring.

CHAPTER 3

I CAN'T #&$%! SLEEP!

Sleep problems are a common issue that many service members are forced to deal with after returning from a deployment. For some, the problem may be falling asleep. For others, the problem may be staying asleep. Some may experience disturbing dreams about things they witnessed while on deployment. Whether you have a difficult time reaching that peaceful slumber or completing a few hours of uninterrupted rest or wake up thinking you need to respond to some unidentifiable threat, sleep difficulties can create a tremendous amount of stress and aggravation for you.

Let's take the case of PFC J., who recently returned home after finishing a 12-month tour to Iraq. Ever since his return, he's noticed that it takes him 2 to 3 hours to fall asleep. This in itself is not that big of a deal. However, considering that he rarely gets to bed before midnight and has an 0530 formation every morning, the sleep deprivation is starting to take a toll. For example, he is noticing that he can't concentrate and remember things as well as he used to. He finds himself falling asleep at inappropriate times, like during a safety briefing by the battalion commander. He no longer seems to be motivated to do things when he gets home from work, and he finds himself on the couch watching television instead of meeting friends

> **Quick Fact**
>
> Sleep problems not only cause daytime fatigue but also cause problems at home and work.

at the local hangout. Last but not least, he has a shorter fuse and loses his temper more quickly. As PFC J.'s story illustrates, problems sleeping can cause more than just fatigue. Among other things, they can get you in the doghouse, chewed out in front of your unit, isolated from your friends, and so many extra pushups that your future grandchildren will be sore.

With this being said, the goals for this chapter are simple. First, we want you to understand what's normal and what's not so normal as far as your sleep is concerned. Second, you will learn some sleep tips and techniques to help you get back on track and gain control over your nights—or days, if you've been stuck working the night shift.

SLEEP DEPRIVATION IS THE NORM

Sleep deprivation in the military is as familiar to the service member as the effective range of an M16 rifle (550 meters, for those who were sleeping during the weapons class). Service members are required to pull seemingly never-ending guard duty, participate in long and tedious training and combat missions, bunk with often noisy and obnoxious roommates, and—for whatever unknown reason—muster 3 hours before anything is scheduled. Not to mention the all-nighters where the Red Bull flows like water and the sounds of Halo echo throughout the barracks halls. Point being, you have learned to

> **Quick Fact**
>
> The average person needs around 7 to 8 hours of sleep each night.

function on less sleep than your civilian counterparts. But the key word is *function,* which does not equal optimal performance (or even adequate performance). There will be consequences . . . some dire. That whole thing about how you only need 4 hours of sleep a night is not true. Sure, it's fine in a combat zone for a short period of time, but it won't cut it for the long term. Most people need 7 to 8 hours on a regular basis, and that includes you.

When you don't get enough sleep, you are at greater risk of injury and death because of a decrease in your time to react physically and mentally to a dangerous situation in the combat zone. You may have trouble making quick decisions and thinking through problems that need immediate solutions. In the garrison environment, you put yourself at increased risk of motor vehicle accidents, training mishaps, and upsetting your first sergeant, gunnery sergeant, or chief. Moreover, you will be less efficient, less motivated, less optimistic, and probably less fun to be around. So, how do you fix all this?

WHAT TO EXPECT AFTER GETTING BACK

Experts, many of whom have also deployed themselves, will tell you that it takes anywhere from 3 to 6 months to get used to your old life after returning from a deployment. Service members typically report two general problems regarding sleep once they get back: difficulty falling asleep and waking up during the night from bad dreams. The good news is that these problems are expected and normal . . . to an extent. The even better news is that there are things you can do to fix the problem.

PROBLEMS GETTING TO SLEEP: WHAT'S CAUSING THEM AND WHAT CAN YOU DO?

Readjusting to garrison or shore life can be a challenge. Loved ones' expectations may be high, which may lead to disappointments. Things in your love life may have changed while you were gone. The decision of whether to stay in the military or become a civilian causes uncertainty and anxiety. How to pay $2,000 worth of bills with only $1,500 perplexes you. If you are experiencing any of these or related issues, you may be ruminating. In other words, you are constantly thinking or worrying about the problem. Rumination is the number one culprit when it comes to not being able to get to sleep. As you can likely relate, many people think about how to fix problems while lying in bed. Hey—it's quiet and you've got nothing else to do. Right? The issue with this is that you can't sleep if you are running every possible scenario through your head about how to solve your relationship, financial, and work problems or worrying about what you need to do the next day. Before you know it, hours have passed. Furthermore, you are likely stressing yourself out even more, making it difficult to relax and fall asleep.

Another common culprit or, more accurately, group of culprits, is bad sleep habits. During your deployment, you likely developed some behaviors that make it a challenge to sleep well. Behaviors such as staying up late watching television or playing video games, exercising, eating, using tobacco or caffeine, and getting into heated discussions with family or friends shortly before trying to sleep are prime examples. Finally, common problems such as depression and

> ## Quick Fact
>
> Bad sleep habits such as watching TV or playing video games in bed contribute to sleep problems.

anxiety can make it difficult to receive that much needed rest you so desperately seek. So, now what?

FIVE STEPS FOR GETTING TO SLEEP

Deal With Any Major Stress Left Over From Earlier in the Day

Write down your thoughts and feelings about what's been bothering you. Talk with a friend about your problems. Schedule a late appointment with the chaplain or, as you might guess, with a psychologist. Do something to set your mind at ease so you can be rested for whatever happens tomorrow.

Stop Thinking About Things When You Are in Bed

Instead, set aside time each evening, and do nothing but worry. Typically, 30 minutes will do the trick. This may sound strange, but it works. One of two things will likely happen. You will either reach some decision about your situation or you will realize how ridiculous it is to lose sleep over the problem and postpone thinking about it until tomorrow. If that doesn't work, make yourself think about something else. Think about a place you would like to go on vacation. Think about something relaxing you have done in the past, and relive it in your mind. Make a conscious effort not to think about the things that keep playing over and over in your head, and soon you'll be able to switch channels in your mind fairly easily and get to sleep.

Use the Bed for Only Two Things . . . Sleep and Sex

Whenever you do other things in bed, such as watching television, reading, or playing video games, you are associating the bed with something other than sleep. So, when you get into bed because you are ready to go to sleep, your body and mind are gearing up to spend the next few hours watching television because this is what you have taught them that the bed is for. Using the bed only for sleep retrains your mind and body. Also, if you are not able to fall asleep within 15 to 20 minutes, get up and do something else for a little while. But don't do anything too interesting—fold the laundry or start a chapter in a textbook (who knows, maybe this book would be good for that). Again, the bed is for sleeping and sex.

Use the Hour or Two Before Bed as a Time to Let Your Mind and Body Calm Down

Now is not the time to run sprints on the treadmill, eat a big, spicy burrito, or get into an argument with your boyfriend or girlfriend. Prepare yourself for sleep. Prebed routines can be helpful. Read the kids a bedtime story, take a hot shower, make lunch for the next day, or do whatever you want. Just do the same thing each night so that your body and brain can get a clue as to what is coming next.

Avoid Caffeine and Tobacco Late in the Evening

Don't drink caffeinated beverages for at least 4 hours before bedtime, and stay away from the tobacco for at least 30 minutes. Seriously, don't let the last things you do before bed be finishing off a Mountain Dew and snuffing out a Marlboro 100. Both substances increase heart rate and respiration, which is not good if you are looking to go to sleep anytime soon.

WAKING UP FROM BAD DREAMS: WHAT'S CAUSING THEM AND WHAT CAN YOU DO?

If you are having nightmares, you are certainly not alone. Virtually every human will have a nightmare at least once in his or her lifetime, and experts have shown that as many as 25% of people have a nightmare at least once a month. Considering how common nightmares are and how disturbing they can be to the dreamer, these nighttime spoilers can create a lot of unneeded stress in a service member's life. Although the actual nightmares may seem harmless to the waking person, they can create a number of secondary concerns such as interrupted and unrefreshing sleep, depressed mood, and decreased functioning during the day. Obviously, you don't need this added aggravation.

HOW TO PUT THE NIGHTMARES TO REST

As a result of having been deployed to a hostile environment, you are at increased risk of bad dreams. Not only were you living in a dangerous place and hearing daily stories of horrific events, many of you were also outside the wire living those events. Some of this stuff has stayed with you. So, what do you do?

Quick Fact
Nightmares after returning from deployment are not unusual. However, it's important to seek help when they affect your ability to work or play.

**Remind Yourself That Bad Dreams Are Normal
and Common Among Those Returned From Deployment**

For a fair number of you, the nightmares will disappear on their own.
For the rest, you can get a handle on them with a little help.

Think of Pleasant and Positive Events Before Sleep

Experts have shown that what we are thinking about before falling
asleep can be connected to what we dream about: using a computer
analogy, "garbage in during wakefulness = garbage out during sleep."

Overcome the Fear of Going Back to Sleep

Many who suffer nightmares on a frequent basis report fears about
going back to sleep after being awakened by a nightmare. Remind
yourself that nightmares can't hurt you and that you can gain control
over this problem.

Keep a Nightmare Journal

Documenting how often, what type, and how disturbing your nightmares are can help you gain a sense of mastery over the situation. It
can also help you determine whether there is a theme to your dreams,
and you can monitor whether they are getting worse, better, or just
staying the same.

Seek Professional Help

Nightmares can be a symptom of a more serious problem, such
as posttraumatic stress disorder, which requires professional help
(see Chapter 12 if you are wondering whether this might be an issue

for you). Consult a mental health professional at your local behavioral health or life skills center. If you would rather not see someone at your local post or base, you can contact militaryonesource.com (1-800-342-9647) for confidential help (for more on this and other resources, see the Appendix).

A FEW FINAL THOUGHTS

The general rule of thumb is, if your sleep situation hasn't started improving after 1 month, you should go check in with someone. If your sleep hasn't returned to normal after about 2 months post-deployment and is not getting any better, you should go check in with someone. Again, this can be a chaplain or a post or base counselor. You don't necessarily need to go to the shrink's office right away. However, there are some damned fine psychologists and psychiatrists in the military, and it doesn't hurt to make them earn their money.

CHAPTER 4

THE DEPLOYMENT WIPED ME OUT FINANCIALLY

Financial problems are unfortunately a common problem for today's military members, particularly with the recent dramatic changes to the nation's overall economy. Gas prices go up and down, food is more expensive, and civilian spouses are having a harder time finding jobs given the rise in unemployment. Combine this with service members' increased risk of financial problems because they spend so much time away, and the outcome can be terrible.

Perhaps you've been deployed for 6, 7, 9, 12, 15, or more months. If you are on regular active duty, you've probably been collecting extra money that is tax exempt by being in a hostile fire area or collecting sea pay or some other extra income. This means that you should have either some healthy savings when you get home or at least less debt. Maybe you are a reservist or guardsman who had to leave a job to deploy, and your income went down. Or maybe your spouse was laid off while you were deployed, causing a significant decrease in funds or increase in debt while you were gone. Maybe he or she didn't say anything to you so that you wouldn't be stressed out while you were deployed. Imagine returning from deployment to find serious financial problems. These problems may range from credit card debt, loss of savings, home foreclosure, mismanaged funds, or

> **Quick Fact**
>
> Financial problems can affect anyone in the military, from the youngest to the most experienced.

even the loss of personal property, sold without your knowledge while you were deployed. In this chapter, we address some of the common financial problems experienced by service members when they return from deployment and discuss how to manage those problems.

Consider these service members:

- LCPL A. had been married for 3 months. She got a power of attorney (a legal document that gives another person the authority to make decisions for you while you are gone) giving her new husband control of her assets. He sold her car and her jewelry and spent every cent of her income while she served in Iraq for 7 months. When she returned from deployment, he was gone, and she was left not only with an empty bank account, no car, and no jewelry but also with $23,000 in credit card debt. He was nowhere to be found.
- SGT B. had been dating his girlfriend for 2 years. They had plans to get married when he returned from deployment, and he trusted her with his money. They opened a joint account so that she could pay his bills while he was deployed to Afghanistan. SGT B.'s girlfriend wasn't the best with a budget, and she quickly began spending his extra income while he was gone. Although she did manage to pay his bills, he came home to an empty bank account.
- Lt. Col. C., a reservist, was deployed for 15 months to Afghanistan. He left a higher paying job to serve. However,

with his wife's income, the family was still in a good financial position. Unfortunately, his wife was laid off 4 months into his deployment, and he returned to find letters threatening foreclosure on his home and $40,000 in credit card debt.

- PVT D. signed his power of attorney over to his mother while he deployed for 15 months. She was supposed to save the money so that he could buy a car when he got back from deployment. While he was gone, however, his brother convinced his mother to pay his (the brother's) bills. She spent all of PVT D.'s income while he was deployed, and he returned home to no money for a car. In addition, his family was angry with him because he did not want to continue financially supporting his brother.

- LCDR E. had been married for 7 years. He and his wife had no children, unless you count the dog. And LCDR E. definitely loved that dog. He went on a routine shipboard deployment for 6 months and came home to find his wife had moved out, the dog was in the pound, and only $500 was left of his entire life's savings.

Sound painfully familiar? What do you do now?

STEP 1: DAMAGE CONTROL

Although you may be experiencing a variety of emotions, none of them pleasant and all of them strong, you have to set that aside and protect yourself from further problems. Depending on your situation, this may require legal assistance and guidance from a financial professional and help from your chain of command. As military members, a smart and resourceful group of people, we may be reluctant to seek help for a problem. Adopt that strategy in this case, and the situation is only going to get worse.

If there is a legal situation at hand (divorce, theft, home fore-closure, etc.), you need to go to base or post legal immediately. Legal will be able to guide and advise you on a variety of issues, such as canceling the power of attorney. If you have an issue that military legal cannot help you with, they will be able to tell you where you can get assistance.

You should then go to the financial advisor or counselor at your command, and tell them what's going on. This will enable them to help you protect your remaining assets and your credit, stop further unnecessary spending or debt accumulation, provide assistance in obtaining emergency financial relief in some cases, and eventually get you back on track with regards to your financial goals. Swallow your pride here and lay it all out on the table.

You should also let your chain of command know what happened. This will help your command to support you and protect you from a variety of repercussions, such as assisting you if creditors send letters to your command or if your security clearance is jeopardized (you can lose your clearance because of debt).

STEP 2: GAIN A HEALTHY PERSPECTIVE

Now that you have protected yourself from further financial problems, allow yourself to be angry, depressed, or whatever emotion you want. Then get over it (yes, that's right, suck it up). This recommendation probably sounds unlikely coming from a couple of psychologists, but the reality is that it doesn't help you, and the longer you allow

---

Quick Fact

Financial problems are best managed by seeking support from professionals.

---

yourself to be driven by your emotions, the worse the outcome will be for you.

Okay, that's easy to say, and maybe it even makes sense, but maybe that's easier said than done. How do you do it? Hit the gym, go for long runs, actively work to improve the situation, talk out the situation with friends, and above all don't be your own worst enemy. Don't ride your motorcycle at high speeds or drink yourself into a stupor (for more on anger, see Chapter 2 of this book).

Sometimes when bad things happen to us, we respond in ways that aren't good for us. Sometimes we take all of the blame, even if that is not rational. For example, when something like this happens, some people think, "I must be an idiot" or "My life is over." These are what we call *irrational beliefs,* and they must be actively disputed. Dispute them by examining the evidence that supports or doesn't support each thought.

Evidence in support of "I must be an idiot":

- You failed to protect your money.
- You may have made a bad decision about whom to leave in control of your money.

Evidence not in support of "I must be an idiot":

- You are a military member who is trusted with protecting other people.
- This has happened to enough people that we wrote a chapter in a book about it.

Other people might think, "My life is over." Psychologists call this *catastrophizing.* Translating this into commonsense talk, it basically means overreacting. Again, examine the evidence.

> **Quick Fact**
>
> Irrational thoughts can lead to irrational actions.

Evidence in support of "My life is over":

- Umm—there isn't any.

Evidence not in support of "My life is over":

- You aren't dying.
- Financial problems are reversible.
- If you are staying in, you still have a job and an income and are on the path to fixing the problem.

When you are in control of your emotions, it's time for the next step.

STEP 3: DEAL WITH THE RELATIONSHIP PROBLEM

If someone spent all of your money while you were deployed or didn't communicate with you regarding the finances, don't fool yourself; there is a relationship problem that needs to be fixed or at least managed. Maybe you already did this in Step 1 by ending the relationship or maybe the person who did this left you. If so, then things will be worked out in a divorce or breakup (if this is an issue for you, take a look at Chapter 5).

Maybe ending the relationship is not in your plans; maybe the financial problems are not anyone's fault and are simply a reflection of today's economic problems, or maybe the person in question is a relative. If the person in question is a spouse or significant other, and the behavior was not a result of poor budgeting skills or non-preventable financial problems because of spouse job loss, you should probably go talk to a relationship counselor or a chaplain. Let's face it, money is one of those topics that creates significant tension for couples. And couples who are willing to seek assistance to learn to discuss money matters without fighting are more likely to work things out. Please know this: Fixing a relationship in which one or both parties have violated the basic trust of the relationship is very hard and requires a lot of work from both people. It is doable, but you need to work on it as hard as if you were training for a mission. If the person who mismanaged your funds was a relative (e.g., a parent), you need to decide on the best course of action to take. It may just be best to find someone else to take care of your financial matters when you deploy again.

STEP 4: MAKE SURE THIS NEVER HAPPENS AGAIN

Before your next deployment, make a plan for your money. It is recommended that all service members draw up an updated will and power of attorney before they deploy. Take advantage of these free services, and get advice from a financial counselor before you go see the lawyer. A financial counselor or advisor is the best person to advise you, but here are some things to think about. Do you need to sign over a power of attorney? If not, don't do it. Or, if absolutely necessary, consider a limited power of attorney (e.g., just for your car). Get help from a financial advisor or counselor to help you make these decisions on the basis of your personal circumstances. Can your bills be paid automatically through your bank? If so, do it—you don't have to rely on anyone. This is highly recommended regardless of whether

> **Quick Fact**
>
> Most financial problems can be prevented by good planning and communication.

or not you are currently deployed. Was the problem related to a significant other who did not possess good budgeting skills? If so, work on the budget together while you are home, so that your significant other is better at it the next time, and make sure he or she has resources available for assistance while you are gone (like the financial counselor on base or post).

Last, on most deployments service members have at least intermittent access to the Internet or phone. You don't want to be overly concerned with things not focused on the mission, but you will have occasion to check your bank or credit card balance. You should also have an opportunity to set up a system to communicate with your spouse or other person taking care of the finances on a fairly regular basis or if an unexpected major purchase has to be made.

STEP 5: LET OTHERS LEARN FROM YOUR MISTAKES

The best thing about making mistakes, especially big ones, is that we aren't usually prone to making the same mistake again. In the military, however, we have an obligation to our peers and to those who serve under us to also protect them from similar mistakes. We know that military members are at risk of others taking advantage or making mistakes that aren't in their best interests because they have to go away so often. As you progress through the ranks, help your subordinates and peers put plans that protect them into place.

A FEW FINAL THOUGHTS

Returning from deployment to find your money gone is only one of the monetary risks service members face. Payday loans and actions by other predatory lenders and, in the case of junior members, a lack of financial experience are also significant risks. In addition, reservists and guardsmen, who may have to take a pay cut when they get activated, face a variety of unique problems. In today's economy, military members must proactively address financial planning, address financial problems early, and use the multitude of resources available through the military. Fixing financial problems may take a while, but it is doable, and your command is there to assist you. Please see the Appendix for financial planning and education resources.

CHAPTER 5

IT LOOKS LIKE I'M GOING TO BE SINGLE AGAIN

You've heard about sailors who are served divorce papers after stepping onto the pier after a 6-month deployment. You've heard about service members who came home to find their spouse living with another person. You probably know someone who came home to find a spouse pregnant with someone else's baby. And you might also know someone who came home to find their girlfriend or boyfriend married to someone else. We're sure you've heard stories of your own, and if you are reading this chapter, you probably have one yourself. Divorce, marital separation, and relationship breakups can happen to anyone, and they are always rough to deal with. In the military, however, particularly after a deployment, it can be extra hard, especially if your spouse, boyfriend, or girlfriend did not give you any indication that this was an issue either before or during your deployment.

Depending on what the issue is for you, you will have a number of emotional, legal, and financial problems to deal with. In this chapter, we discuss those problems and provide some guidance on how to manage them. We'll talk about the emotional issues first because successful control of these will help a lot with your financial and legal decision making and keep you out of trouble.

> **Quick Fact**
>
> You are not in this alone. There are a lot of resources in the military to help you work through a breakup.

KEEPING YOUR COOL AND YOUR SANITY AFTER A BREAKUP

Breakups are never easy, but being dumped while you are on deployment seriously sucks. Some say it's like being run over by a truck or being on a roller coaster with no end. You are going to feel some strong emotions, the most common of which are confusion, anger, numbness, shock, and sadness. You will want to know why. You might want to scream and threaten. You might want to hurt someone. You might think about crawling into a bottle or just not want to leave your house. You might even think about hurting yourself (if this is the case, please get help right away; Chapter 14 can guide you). You've got to deal with this stuff first and foremost before you start making any decisions about your children or your property. Here are some tips for managing your emotions and avoiding bad decisions.

Talk It Out With Someone

To start the process of getting back on track, talk with someone about what's going on, but not your soon-to-be ex. Talk with a friend, your first sergeant or chief, a counselor, your mother—whoever is that person in your life who listens, gives you good advice, and isn't afraid to tell you when you aren't thinking straight. Talking with someone who has made it through a breakup is also a good idea. If you and your ex share the same set of friends, this can make getting the support you both need difficult. If you need to vent or talk things out with someone, don't do it with someone who may also be a primary support for your spouse.

Know That Your Ex Is Not a Support System

You should not attempt to use your ex as a support system. In fact, we recommend not engaging in any unnecessary conversations with your ex until you are in control of your emotions. Obviously, if you have children or a financial issue that needs to be resolved, you will need to talk to your ex about these issues. But do not engage in any talk about the breakup right away. Talking with him or her too early will likely only get you more worked up than you are now.

Consider Your Children Before You Say Anything to Your Soon-to-Be Ex

Although interactions with your spouse should be kept to a minimum, if you have children there is no way to avoid communication. Keep in mind that your children are stuck in the middle of this thing. How you behave around your spouse and what you say to each other will have profound effects on your children for life. Whether this is going to be positive or negative is up to you. Divorce is hard on kids—there's no need to make it harder.

Don't Forget Your Obligations

Although you may be focused on your own feelings and frustration about the relationship, remember that you are still in the military, and your obligations to your command and your family are not

---

Quick Fact

The marriage may be over, but your parenting duties don't end.

---

over. Get yourself organized, and keep your chain of command in the loop. You are going to have appointments during the work day, and you are going to be distracted by your thoughts and feelings about the breakup. You are going to need support. Try to minimize this impact by doing what you would normally do with appointments (e.g., schedule around duty days), and never forget that with every decision you make regarding the divorce, your children need to be the first consideration.

Take a Step Back

After you have started talking this out and working through it, take a step back. Let's face it, when we are angry or depressed, we don't think straight. The part of our brain that ramps up our emotions is set on high, and the part of our brain that helps us think rationally is in the off or low setting. Don't make any major decisions; take some time to think things through. A couple of days of getting your act together will go a long way toward making things better for you.

No Ex Sex

When couples are fighting, there are a lot of strong emotions on both sides. Although this may not make sense, sometimes this leads to a little temporary passion, if you know what we mean. Please, don't allow yourself to be seduced by your ex (and don't try to seduce your ex either). Sex between people who are going through a divorce is a bad idea and will only serve to prolong your painful emotions related to the break up. There'll be sex for you later, once your divorce is finalized, and it will be in the context of a more fulfilling relationship. Trust us—a few minutes of feeling good isn't worth the emotional fallout, and sex won't fix your relationship.

Take Care of Yourself

In addition to relying on friends and talking this out, take care of yourself. All of the healthy lifestyle things you already know about are very important right now (eat right; exercise; get good sleep; lay off the alcohol, gambling, or drugs; and spend time with good friends who know what's going on with you). In addition to the general things to do to keep yourself functioning at a reasonable level, set some realistic goals for yourself to help take the focus off of the bad stuff that's going on and refocus it onto something good. Take a college class, knock 10 seconds off of your run time, or teach your son or daughter to swim the backstroke. Actively tell yourself that your life hasn't ended just because your relationship is over.

In addition to doing things that are good for you, avoid those things that aren't. Now is not the time to slack off on exercise, start chain smoking, go through a 12-pack a night, or start eating pizza twice a day. When we are stressed about anything, we are more likely to make bad decisions, make mistakes, and even get sick. Don't go driving at high speeds or by your ex's house in the middle of the night, or other stupid things we sometimes do when we are really upset and our feelings are hurt. If you are having problems dealing with your anger, please read Chapter 2. In other words, don't defeat yourself.

Learn to think straight: When we've taken an emotional hit, sometimes we actively make it worse. Remember that sometimes when bad things happen to us, we respond in ways that aren't good for us. Sometimes we take all of the blame, even if that is not rational. Following are some examples of unrealistic or irrational thoughts.

- I'm no good, or I'm not good enough.
- It's all my fault.
- I'll never find someone as good as him or her again.
- My life is over.

Quick Fact

The way you think about things controls how you feel about them.

If any of those kinds of thoughts are in your head, replace them now! Although it may be hard at first, look at this as a challenge and learning opportunity and let it go. It can take a while, but you have to make a conscious decision to move on. This relationship might be over, but you are a military stud or studette (okay, we made that up), and there is fun and love in your future. Some healthy thinking here might be:

- There are plenty of fish in the sea.
- Having had a relationship that didn't work out will make my next relationship better. I will be able to choose better and not make the same mistakes.
- I am a service member, which means that I am strong. I can get over this and move on with my life.

LEGAL ISSUES

First, we want to be clear that we aren't lawyers. If you are looking for legal advice, please don't think you will find it here. This is a brief discussion of some things that come up for service members. If you are having a messy divorce or a complicated one because you have children, you believe your spouse is requesting unrealistic compensation, or you have been married a long time, for example, you need a lawyer who has experience working with military divorce. If you have been married briefly, don't have kids, and no one is disagreeing about anything, you might be able to make do with a mediator or other person to help you. If you are getting a divorce, here are some things to think about. If you can't answer these questions, you should go see a lawyer.

- Where are you going to get divorced? This can be tricky because of residency and jurisdiction issues as well as different state laws about things such as alimony, child custody, and property distribution.
- Who is getting custody of the children? What will the visitation rights be? How much child support will you have to pay? These issues can become very contentious and result in a lot of fighting between divorcing spouses. The service member is likely to feel at a serious disadvantage here because it is hard to compete for custody with a nondeploying spouse.

Also keep in mind that the military considers you to be married until the day you are divorced. Don't start dating anyone or move in with some other romantic interest until you are actually divorced. If things blow up, the military could say you are committing adultery. There might be some exceptions to this rule depending on the type of divorce you are getting (e.g., a no-fault divorce), but you need to check this out with your lawyer. Please also note, it is generally not a good idea to get involved in another relationship right away anyway—you need time to get your head back on straight.

Some people are in a hurry to get the divorce over with. Some even try to get divorced in other countries where you can theoretically get a quickie divorce. The military has too many rules about service members and divorce—so don't try to do this. It could lead to significant legal and financial consequences for you.

Another thing to know is that generally you can't have a lawsuit filed against you while you are deployed overseas; this includes divorce. If something weird is going on while you are deployed,

---

> **Quick Fact**
>
> If you need a lawyer, get one who is trained in military divorce laws and regulations.

contact the judge advocate general (JAG) who is assigned to your unit (there is always a JAG out there—get some help from your chain of command to access one).

FINANCIAL AND PROPERTY ISSUES

Money can be a major issue when people are getting divorced, and although it hurts to give money to someone who hurt you and who maybe even cheated on you, you may have to, depending on the circumstances. Even though you may be angry, don't forget that there are a lot of laws in place to protect spouses, and if you aren't doing what you need to, your spouse can call your command and make you or can drag you through court, costing you a ton in legal fees. Don't go there. Also, in the middle of a divorce it can be hard to motivate yourself to deal with some of these issues. Don't sit around and do nothing either—that will also make everything worse. Last, don't be in too much of a hurry. Do what you need to do; don't give in to a bunch of unrealistic or ill-informed requests just because you want it to be over. Instead, educate yourself about the rules in your state and in the military so that you can make the best decisions for everyone involved. Here is some general information that will help guide you in figuring out what you need to ask your lawyer or get more information about.

- If you have a prenuptial agreement, this likely trumps any other laws about property during a divorce.

- Your dependents are entitled to your basic allowance for subsistence (BAS).
- If you have served 20 years or more, your spouse is entitled to some of your retirement pay if you were married at least 10 years while you were serving. It is important to understand that the judge in your divorce can award your ex more if it is warranted. It is also important to understand that your ex may still be entitled to some of your retirement even if you divorce before you retire.
- While the divorce is getting processed, your spouse keeps his or her military privileges (base, medical, commissary, etc.). Your spouse will probably lose these benefits as soon as the divorce is finalized, unless you have been married a long time, usually 20 years. Your children retain their benefits.
- Your military pay and retirement are not your only financial assets, and you need to have these organized. Get all of your documentation together regarding any assets (house, stocks, bank accounts, Servicemembers Group Life Insurance, etc.) and debt (credit cards, loans, etc.), and discuss these with your lawyer.
- A divorce will affect you financially in a number of ways. Depending on your situation, you may need professional help. A financial counselor will be able to help you with issues such as taxes, retirement, credit, and budgeting.

A FEW FINAL THOUGHTS

Ending a relationship stinks. People get hurt, and when people are angry or depressed they sometimes do things that aren't in their best interests. Divorce in particular causes a lot of problems if the breakup is not a mutual decision and if one or both of the parties involved feels betrayed. Add kids into the mix, and the situation gets even trickier.

If you are having a messy divorce, please get a lawyer specializing in military divorce (the rules are too different to get someone who doesn't know what he or she is doing), and don't make any decisions without talking to your attorney.

Above all, remember that your children are innocent bystanders to whatever is happening; you must keep your cool around them and be able to get along with your ex. If you cannot do this, you risk scarring them emotionally, and this cannot be tolerated. No divorce needs to be messy, and there are a lot of supports in place to make divorces less stressful for everyone. As with everything, if you are having problems controlling your emotions or just feel stuck in a rut, a military counselor or mental health provider can probably get you on the right track in just a few sessions. Divorces are hard, but there is no reason to make them harder. If you can get control of your emotions, your divorce will be shorter, easier, cheaper, and less emotionally damaging than if you let yourself be controlled by your feelings.

CHAPTER 6

MY CHILD HAS CHANGED

The title of this chapter describes a common complaint from service members after they have returned from a deployment. You've been gone for many months, and you want nothing more than to spend time with your wonderful and loving children. But when you get home, you find out that the security guard stationed outside the Old Navy store at the local mall has more authority over your 5-year-old than you do. Or the teenager whom you were always doing things with before you deployed looks at you as though you have the plague. It's certainly understandable why this is frustrating.

One common theme that you will likely notice throughout this book is that things change. As other chapters explain, you are not the same person you were before you deployed. For example, it's likely that your views about life have shifted. Your spouse or significant other is probably not the same either. He or she may have become more independent or developed new interests and hobbies during your absence. Your children are no different. Children of service members have unique challenges. Not only do they have to learn to deal with a parent being sent off to some remote and distant country for months on end, but they also have to deal with the real possibility of never

---

Quick Fact
Children grow and change a lot while you are deployed.

seeing that parent again. On top of that, children grow both mentally and physically during a deployment and truly are not the same people they were when their parent left. When you combine this with children's disappointment with missed birthdays, Little League games, and graduations, you create a perfect storm for hurt feelings on their part. Consequently, your child may act differently toward you, which can make the homecoming a stressful experience as opposed to a joyous occasion.

The goal of this chapter is to help you understand that your child has changed since you left for deployment. This doesn't mean that he or she has morphed into some strange and foreign being, but rather that he or she has gotten older; been exposed to new experiences; and grown physically, mentally, and psychologically. In meeting this goal, we discuss what's to be expected and typical in how children may act after the military parent returns home. We also discuss the red flags to look out for as far as your child's behavior is concerned. Finally, we provide you with some tips and techniques for managing potential disruptive and defiant behavior that your child may be exhibiting.

One last note: Each and every child is different. The information we provide is in general terms; what is normal for one child may not be normal for another. You know your child better than anyone else, so make sure to rely on the parental judgment that has gotten you this far. Keep this in mind, and you will most certainly get things back on track.

WHAT CAN YOU EXPECT?

The one sure thing you can count on is that your child has changed. For some children, the change will be minor and largely unrelated to your deployment. An example would be a 2-year-old who just loves to say "no" to everything. This is most likely not the result of some repressed anger and resentment about your leaving but because saying no gives the 2-year-old some control over his or her world. This is a normal stage of development. Therefore, it's important to keep a realistic perspective when you think about your child's behavior. Not everything your child does that concerns you or hurts your feelings is related to the deployment.

It's also important to keep in mind that how the child responds to the deployment is dependent in part on the child's age. Take preschoolers, for example. For these youngsters, being separated from a parent during a deployment can be very confusing. It may take them longer to warm up to the returning parent. Think about it. They remember you leaving, couldn't fully grasp why you left, and now all of a sudden you are back. That would be confusing to anyone. Moreover, for those of you who have children around age 1 or younger, it's possible they don't even remember you. Don't feel bad about this. It's an issue of brain development, not a reflection on your parenting skills.

School-age children are a little different. You may find that your 6-, 8-, or 10-year-old is very clingy and desperately in need of attention. In these situations, most likely an adequate attachment developed between you and your child before the deployment. What's possibly happening now is that your child is fearful that you will leave again and is showing you how important you are to him or her. This is good in that it is a sign of a healthy child–parent relationship, and it will just take some time and patience to set things right again.

> ### Quick Fact
>
> Teenagers tend to be loyal to the parent who stayed behind.

Those of you with teenagers at home are well aware that this group is a completely different animal. They may seem moody (more so than usual), act as though they couldn't care less that you are home, or be openly hostile toward you. Teenagers tend to be very loyal to the parent who stayed behind. They may reject your attempts at discipline and blame you for everything that went wrong with the family while you were away. Obviously, this can be heartbreaking for a parent who already feels guilty about leaving.

The good news is that much of this behavior will lessen and disappear with time. Just like your marriage, job, and social life, this too will get better. However, there are things you can do to speed up the process. But first, let's talk about the red flags.

WATCHING FOR THE RED FLAGS

As discussed in the previous section, much of the behavior your child is showing is normal and expected. Change is a part of life, and you shouldn't lose too much sleep over it. However, some behaviors should alert you to problems that are more serious.

Preschoolers (Ages 1–5)

The younger a child is, the tougher it is to figure out what's going on with him or her. Take 2-year-olds, for example. Generally, it's not until ages 18 to 24 months that a child is able to string three words together to make a sentence. Obviously, the less verbal a child is, the more difficult it will be for them to communicate what's going on. This is why being aware of nonverbal behavior is so important for parents. In younger children, particularly those who aren't talking much yet, the parent should be aware of unexplained crying or tearfulness. Most children this age can be soothed and comforted by the parent. An inability to calm or soothe the child may indicate a problem that requires attention from a medical or mental health professional. Another problem to be aware of in younger preschoolers is a change in eating habits. A refusal to eat may indicate not only an attachment or trust issue but also potential medical problems. In older preschoolers (i.e., 3- to 5-year-olds), the more serious problems to look for are sleep disturbances, such as an inability to fall asleep or bad dreams; increased acts of aggression and violence toward people, animals, or toys; or prolonged withdrawal from family members and playmates. Most child experts agree that sudden-onset aggressive and violent behavior in children is a sign of something serious.

School-Age Children (Ages 6–12)

School-age children will be more vocal about what's going on with them . . . generally. Although they may not fully understand exactly what's wrong, they are able to communicate to you that life has gotten hard and that they are struggling. So, listen to them. Don't disregard their complaints. In many cases, this is all it takes. With that being said, there are behaviors that should alert you to the possibility that something more serious is going on. School-age children who are dealing with high levels of stress will more frequently complain of physical problems. For example, they will report headaches or stomachaches. Some children will display acting-out behavior at school, such as talking back to the teacher or getting into fights with other students. Others will display an open hostility toward one or both parents, but most likely toward the parent returning from

> **Quick Fact**
>
> A headache or stomachache in a school-age child could be an expression of sadness or anger.

deployment. Remember, don't take this personally. This is the point at which keeping things in perspective and acknowledging that your child does not truly hate you will get you down this river, even in your paddleless boat.

Teenagers (Ages 13–18)

In general, teenagers can be difficult. Almost any parent of a teen can expect random mood swings, some level of defiance, and behavior that can only be described as strange. However, there are some behaviors in teens that should raise a red flag for the parent. Similar to preschoolers, teens have a tendency to be nonverbal, particularly when it comes to interacting with parents. This tendency is the result not of a lack of a vocabulary, as is the case with young children, but of some teenage law that has frustrated parents since the beginning of time. Regardless, parents should be concerned if they notice their teen withdrawing from friends, family, and activities that he or she used to enjoy (e.g., sports, going to the movies) or a sudden change in grades. Parents should be concerned if they notice a drop in the teen's self-esteem or an increase in self-criticism. Comments such as "I'm ugly," "I'm fat," or "I can never do anything right" should be taken seriously. Sure, many teens will make these types of comments at some point. Nevertheless, this is where you have to use your parenting judgment to figure out if the comments have become more frequent or if your teen seems to become overly upset when he or she

---

Quick Fact

Don't be afraid to talk to your child about suicide.

---

says these things. Last, if your teenager, or any age child for that matter, ever makes a comment about suicide or wanting to die, take them to see a professional immediately. If your child has not made specific comments about suicide, but you feel something is just not quite right, ask whether he or she is having thoughts of hurting him- or herself. The idea that talking about suicide with your child will put the thought into her or his head is just simply wrong.

The teen years can be very difficult. Think back to when you were that age. Keep the lines of communication open, and don't be afraid to ask the tough questions and make the difficult decisions.

BRINGING THINGS BACK INTO BALANCE

Getting things back to normal with your child is not as hard as you may think. For the most part, it just takes a little patience, common sense, and the willingness to be flexible or, as they say in the military, adapt and overcome or *semper Gumby*. Keep in mind that not every tip or technique will work with every child. As we have mentioned before, it is important to rely on your parental instincts. Nobody knows your child better than you. With that said, here are a few things that will help.

Preschoolers

Relying on your parenting intuition and not being afraid to be a kid once in a while will go a long way with preschoolers.

BE THE CARETAKER. Taking over the role of caretaker for a while will help build trust. If you typically don't bathe, feed, dress, read the bedtime story, or tuck your child into bed at night, now is the time to start. Research has shown that providing direct care to a young child builds attachment relatively quickly.

KEEP THEM CLOSE. Younger children need to know that you are truly here. For the first few weeks, keep them in your line of sight. Or better yet, make sure you are in their line of sight. With time and consistency, they will learn that mommy or daddy is truly back.

REASSURE THEM THAT YOU ARE HERE TO STAY. Kids of any age can worry about mom or dad leaving again. For younger children, however, their sense of time is a little off. Young children have a hard time comprehending things far in the future, like a future deployment 12 months away. Let them know that you are back and aren't going anywhere. We do realize that you may have to deploy again in another 6, 12, or 24 months, but talking with your preschool child about this now will do no good.

DRAW, PAINT, OR PLAY A GAME. Art and play are the primary methods of expression for younger children and are typically used by child psychologists when doing child therapy. Spend time painting a picture or playing a board game with your child. During this time, let your child know how much you missed him or her and encourage him or her to express any feelings about your being gone and your being home. Sure, you aren't a child psychologist, but you don't need to be one to help your child adjust to your being back.

School-Age Children

For children of school age, listening, communicating, and acknowledging both positive and negative behaviors are effective.

LISTEN TO THEIR COMPLAINTS. Take their complaints seriously. School-age children have a tendency to complain of physical problems even when the problems are more emotional. Sometimes a tummy ache is a tummy ache, and other times it's not.

IGNORE THE NEGATIVE BEHAVIOR. One of the fastest ways to get a child of this age to stop acting out is to ignore the behavior. This is a core behavioral psychology principle. The more you acknowledge it, the more you reinforce it. If the child is not in danger, let it go.

RECOGNIZE THE POSITIVE BEHAVIOR. Do the exact opposite for positive behavior. When your child does something good, let him or her know it. The best way to make sure the behavior continues is to acknowledge it and be excited by it. Keep in mind that we said *acknowledge* and not *reward*. Rewarding a child can be useful, but it can also teach him or her to expect payment for good deeds.

TALK WITH YOUR CHILD'S TEACHER OR GUIDANCE COUNSELOR. Set up an appointment with your child's teacher or guidance counselor. School professionals are like a second or third parent for many kids. Explain to him or her what kinds of problems you are having with your child. The teacher or guidance counselor may be able to give you some good ideas on how to make things better. You will also be able to find out if there have been any problems or changes noticed at school.

PLAN FOR THE NEXT DEPLOYMENT. It's pretty much a given that if you stay in the military, you will deploy again. There are some things you can do to help younger children while you are away. You can get them a life-sized poster of you that they can see every day. You can video- or audiotape yourself reading several books, and let your spouse play a new one for them every month during your deployment. This gives your child contact with you even though you are gone. There are now a variety of books and even Sesame Street videos that are geared toward helping children understand deployment better. In short, there are a lot of things you can do to make the deployment easier on children, and a little creativity will help your spouse or other caregiver keep you involved with your children, even while you are gone. Please see the Appendix for a list of resources for children.

Teenagers

The teenage years are difficult for any parent. Focus on these tips, and you'll see success.

BE PATIENT AND UNDERSTANDING. Take a deep breath. Don't take things personally. Remind yourself that no child is perfect. Reassure yourself that things will get better. Remember what you were like as a teenager.

GIVE THEM SPACE. Be trusting. Don't crowd your teen. Give teens enough space so that they can become their own person. Remember, they most likely had a significant growth spurt while you were gone as far as independence goes.

GIVE THEM MORE RESPONSIBILITY. This goes along with what we just mentioned. Teens have become more independent. Give them the added responsibility of watching their younger brother, cutting the grass, or making sure the house is locked and secured for the night.

SPEND MORE TIME ALONE WITH THEM. It may seem like an impossible challenge in the beginning, but think back to when you and your teen had something in common. Go fishing or hunting again. Shell out some money to catch a major league game. Have some fun with your teenager.

CONSULT WITH THE SCHOOL GUIDANCE COUNSELOR. If things aren't going well, grades are declining, your teen is withdrawing socially or has started using drugs, or you are concerned about other things going on, call her or his guidance counselor. The guidance counselor is an excellent resource to help you figure out what is bothering your child and deciding whether he or she might need additional help. Because the guidance counselor is someone that most kids in a school already know, it is sometimes easier to get a teenager to talk to the counselor than to a stranger.

A FEW FINAL THOUGHTS

Reuniting with your child after deployment should be a wonderful and hassle-free event. However, for some service members it is a time of disappointment, guilt, and intense frustration. Be patient. Stay calm. Don't take things personally. Show that you care. Use some of the tips provided in this chapter and just be the loving parent that you have always been. However, as always, if things don't get better, go and get help from a doctor or use the resources available at school. Don't forget that teachers and guidance counselors spend a lot of time with your child and are in a good position to help and monitor how things are going.

CHAPTER 7

IS DEPLOYMENT DIFFERENT FOR WOMEN?

There are a lot of questions about women serving in the military, and particularly about women serving in combat zones. We're sure you know that women are not allowed to serve in combat roles. However, this combat exclusion rule for women may be a moot point in the current wars because our front lines are ill defined and women are in places where they are becoming involved in combat action. Nevertheless, some people don't think women can handle the stress of the military, and some people think women should stay home and let the men fight. Other people think women should be able to do everything that men do. These differing opinions about women in today's war have a significant impact on women's day-to-day experience in the military, during deployments, and during that postdeployment adjustment.

Not to mention that there isn't a lot out there to educate deploying women about effectively managing male–female issues in the combat zone. The best advice you got might have been to take a knife with you at all times, always lock your door (if you are fortunate enough to have a door), and never go to the bathroom or shower by

This chapter is written primarily for women but may interest men as well.

Quick Fact
Differing opinions about women in today's war have a significant impact on women's day-to-day experience.

yourself—not exactly comprehensive advice, but definitely reflective of safety issues brought up by the extreme military male-to-female ratio in the war zone and less-than-polite behavior of some of the local employees on base, who may have very different ideas about women than Americans do.

Take the example of LT A. LT A. is a female naval officer who recently returned from Afghanistan. While in country, she had a difficult time dealing with the attitudes of the local men toward women and with being excluded from some physical locations, duties, and meetings because of her gender, while men whom she outranked were performing these duties. To complicate matters, a senior male officer began paying her more attention than she was comfortable with, which evolved into inappropriate sexual remarks and questionable job assignments during the deployment. LT A. believed that because the senior officer was romantically interested in her, he was intentionally and inappropriately keeping her out of locations, convoys, and missions to protect her from potential harm. She felt that the men with whom she was deployed did not see her as an equal because she was unable to do her share of the work. After her return from deployment, she began to question her own self-worth and her decision to join the military and chronically worried about whether she should bring her supervisor's behavior into question. This led to insomnia, which affected her energy level, motivation, and mood.

Before we can talk much about the specifics of LT A.'s case and about addressing women's experiences during and after deployment, it is important to understand the many factors that affect women in the military today. We first take a brief glance at history and then examine some of the challenges that women currently face when serving in the military.

Throughout history, war has had a significant impact on women in the United States and vice versa. During the Civil War, women went to work in ways they had not been allowed to before because most of the men were off fighting the war, and many were killed. They ran businesses and plantations and managed their own property. At least 400 women cross-dressed and fought in the war. The only woman (a doctor named Mary Walker) to have received a Medal of Honor did so in the Civil War. As you know, after the war women were not content to return to their former positions and fought for equal rights. The Civil War provided the means for women to make great strides in obtaining them.

By World War I (WWI), women were starting to serve in the military, mostly as nurses but also as translators, telephone operators, and yeomen. In WWI, 36,000 women served, 200 women were killed, and 80 women were taken prisoner. Unfortunately, although women were working within the military, they did not hold any rank and after the war were not considered to be veterans. This all changed during World War II (WWII), when women began to be recognized for their valuable service on deployments and as pilots. More than 400,000 women served during this war. Women were granted limited rank in WWII, and after the war women achieved a permanent (but restricted) status in the military. After Vietnam, things started to equalize at a more rapid rate, and a lot of the gender restrictions

---

Quick Fact

Women are not fully integrated into the military, and this makes their experiences different from those of men.

---

began to be lifted. Since the end of the Vietnam War, women have achieved integration into 95% of military jobs. Exclusions continue in ground combat roles, submarines, and special forces, but war is once again redefining the role of women in the military.

HOW MUCH OF THE MILITARY IS FEMALE, AND DOES IT MATTER TO YOU?

Approximately 15% of the military is female, although this number varies among the services. The air force has the highest percentage of women, about 20%, and the marines have the lowest, about 6%. The army and navy each have 14%–15%. These small numbers significantly affect a woman's experience while deployed, after deployment, and in the military workplace in general.

First, with only 6% to 20% of your work environment female, normal peer relationships with other women may be infrequent. There will be times when you are the only woman working in a location, attending a meeting, participating in a training evolution, or even living on a forward operating base. These low numbers may be great in the mandatory urinalysis lines where there is never a wait, but as a rule this does make some of the things women normally take for granted more difficult to obtain. And although bonding with your fellow (male) service members is extremely important, being one of a few women singles you out and makes it harder for you to normally integrate into your work environment as a service member.

Another drawback to being female in the military environment is that there aren't many opportunities to have female supervisors, commanders, or mentors. These women truly have opportunities to normalize women's roles in the military and to help you navigate the pitfalls that men don't normally have to deal with (more on that later in this chapter). This includes having that informed female support

---

Quick Fact

Most veteran services are geared toward men.

---

system when you return from deployment. Finally, the military has been addressing the needs of male veterans for a long time, but there isn't the same level of comprehensive services for female veterans yet. So yes, the small number of women in the military significantly affects you as an individual female service member.

CAN WOMEN (I.E., YOU) HACK THE MILITARY?

One of the arguments for keeping women out of the remaining 5% of jobs and truly equalizing military service is that women can't hack it—both physically and psychologically. Although it may be true that the strongest woman will never be as strong as the strongest man, take a look around your units and then tell us that some of the women aren't stronger and faster than some of the men.

But let's take a closer look at the issue of psychologically handling the stressors of military service and particularly deployment. It's true that men and women cope differently with things. Does this mean that women aren't coping well? In some respects, women cope more effectively and less destructively. Women are much less likely than men to cope by using alcohol and are also less likely to violate military or other laws (think bar fights, riding motorcycles recklessly, domestic violence, and other problems). Women also seem to have an edge over men in coping with longer deployments. However, there is also some evidence that women may be more likely than men to develop chronic posttraumatic stress symptoms in the years after traumatic deployments. The reason for this is not yet known. One

75

thing that is known to be a significant predictor of problems is sexual trauma; this is seriously bad news for a woman's mental health both during and after the deployment.

SEXUAL ASSAULT AND HARASSMENT

Sexual assault is a serious problem for military women. Not only do you have to deal with the assault, but that assault may have been by someone whom you believed was essentially a brother-in-arms, a member of your military family. Being so betrayed can create a wide variety of emotions and problems. Sexual assault during a deployment is particularly hard to deal with, and unfortunately any rape can result in posttraumatic stress disorder (PTSD) or other mental health problems such as depression (see the case of HM3 C. in Chapter 12).

Although the rates of military sexual assault are going down, this is still a significant problem warranting much more attention and intervention. In 2002, 3% of military women reported a sexual assault or attempted sexual assault (down from 6% in 1995). It used to be that if you were sexually assaulted and went to a military doctor, it was automatically reported and investigated. Although we think that if you are raped you should definitely report it so that whoever did it can be caught and punished (severely), sometimes people aren't ready for that and want to see a doctor and talk to people confidentially. YOU CAN DO THIS. The military changed this rule in 2005 and no longer requires a mandatory investigation if you seek medical care, to include mental health care after a deployment. In 2007, there were 1,620 service members who reported a sexual assault and who instigated an investigation (called an *unrestricted report*). Of these, 705 service members opted to seek help and not instigate an investigation (called a *restricted report*). One hundred seventy-four assaults were reported in Iraq and Afghanistan while service members

Quick Fact

If you have been sexually assaulted, the military has a lot of resources for you. If you use them, you are less likely to have serious mental health problems because of a sexual assault.

were deployed. It is important to keep in mind that although women are usually the targets of sexual assault, a small number of men in the military are also sexually assaulted.

Fortunately, at least in the arena of sexual assault, the Department of Veterans Affairs is creating new programs for women dealing with military sexual trauma, and there is now a PTSD program that is only for women. If this is something you need, please see the Appendix for information on this program and other programs that might interest you. Please note that any mental health department at any military treatment facility or clinic can also either help you directly or get you tied into the help you need.

In addition to sexual assault, sexual harassment continues to be a problem for military women. Again, as with sexual assault, this is improving. In 1988, 64% of military women reported sexual harassment, whereas in 2002, 24% did. Although this is better, this is still a quarter of all military women! If someone makes a sexually inappropriate comment, gesture, or physical contact, there are a number of things you can do to address it. First, be prepared to confront the person directly. Let the person know frankly that whatever was done was out of your comfort zone and that you would appreciate it if the person did not do it again in the future. Most of the time, this is all it takes to stop an unwanted behavior. Also, by letting people in your workplace know your boundaries, you can prevent the behavior from getting worse.

Looking back at the case of LT A., she did not do this. At the time, she was very stressed out, was working in a combat zone, and opted not to say anything to her senior officer. Her reluctance to say anything at the time is now creating problems for her since returning from deployment. To address her chronic worrying and questions about her own self-worth, she sought treatment from a therapist who encouraged her to address the problem now. She opted to discuss what occurred on deployment face-to-face with the senior officer. He was initially very defensive, but because she had rehearsed what she was going to say with her therapist, she was able to provide concrete examples and did it without emotion or anger. He considered what she had to say and eventually apologized. She was satisfied with his apology, and this enabled her to start moving forward again. Most important, her sleep began to return to normal almost immediately, and she was able to think more clearly about whether to stay in the military.

There were other options for LT A. If she had not been comfortable approaching her senior officer directly, she could also have written a letter or had a third party talk to him. Although her strategy worked for her and the outcome was satisfactory, this may not always be the case. If a behavior is ongoing and doesn't stop, we recommend that you involve your chain of command.

As an aside, it is important to remember that not all sexual comments are sexual harassment. If you don't like something, you should let the other person know, but the reality is that men and women joke around about all kinds of not-politically-correct topics, and this isn't always a bad thing.

STEREOTYPES AND STANDARDS

In addition to restrictions on service, sexual harassment, and sexual assault, stereotypes and standards are also issues that affect a woman's

---

> **Quick Fact**
>
> Gender stereotypes are still a part of the military culture.

military experience. Military men still perceive men as better leaders even though empirical evidence does not support this, and women continue to be held to higher standards than men.

When women began joining the military at incredible rates in WWII (remember, 400,000 women served in WWII), they had to take a test to get in. This was a different test from the one the men had to take, and they were held to a higher standard to get in. Although current Armed Services Vocational Aptitude Battery scores to get in are not standardized on the basis of gender, women are still held to a different standard than men.

Think about this. When you screw something up (hey, we all do it), has anyone ever said that you couldn't succeed because you were a woman? Or when you do something well, have you ever heard, "Wow, that was great for a woman"? When you do something in the military, you are often a woman before you are a master at arms, military police, or parachute rigger. This sounds crazy, but what you do as an individual is what women in the military are being judged on. Whether it is fair or not, you as an individual represent all women in the military.

SO WHAT'S A WOMAN TO DO?

There are many things to do to make your military experience more rewarding, to deal with problems as they arise, and to make the post-deployment adjustment go more smoothly. Make no mistake, there is no way to not consider your gender in your adjustment to returning

79

from deployment. All of the factors we have mentioned affect military women profoundly, but we aren't saying that these obstacles can't be overcome and even used to your advantage. You just have to realize their impact.

Accept That a Woman's Experience in the Military Is Different From a Man's, and Work With It

The reality is that a woman's experience is very different from a man's. It may not be fair, but it is how it is. Always think about the fact that you are a part of history and that you are helping to more fully integrate the military. If these things come up for you, address them responsibly and get mentorship from a more senior woman, even if she isn't in your chain of command. Many commands have become more sensitive to this need and will work to find you a female mentor if you ask.

Address Traumatic and Disturbing Events That Happened Out There Head On

If you were assaulted or harassed in the combat zone and opted not to report it, you can report it now and you can get help now. If this happened and you aren't adjusting back into your old life well, get some professional help and work on finding your way again. A psychotherapist can help you decide how best to address something that happened on deployment. You may choose to address it only in therapy, you may choose a route like LT A.'s, or, if the behavior was severe, you may choose to open an investigation. Although in this chapter we place an emphasis on sexual assault, PTSD and depression are also possible outcomes of other battlefield trauma. Please see Chapter 12 for more information on PTSD and adjusting to having witnessed horrific events.

Address the Philosophical Issues That You Are Experiencing

We've already established that women are not fully integrated into the military. Combine this fact with serving in a combat zone in a Muslim culture that has radically different views of women than in the United States, and it is probable that you have experienced some frustration. Some women are able to shrug this off easily, but it significantly bothers others. If this is an issue for you, you can actively work to educate yourself and become more involved with women's issues. Whether this involves volunteering at a women's shelter, becoming an active mentor of other military women, or giving public talks about serving as a woman in today's military, these types of things can help you tackle philosophical dilemmas and questions.

Reach Out to Other Military Women

Sometimes there aren't a lot of other women around, and sometimes there are none. In the grand scheme of things, there aren't a lot of women who have experienced deployment to a combat zone. But it is important that you have other women to bounce things off of, to socialize with, and to complain to when things are stressful. Network with other local military women and make a routine meeting over coffee or beers—you will be surprised how helpful this can be when navigating the male-dominated organization that you belong to and to assist in your postdeployment transition.

Don't View Your Fellow Service Members as Relationship Prospects While in the Field, and Think Carefully About This When You Get Back

For single women, what better place to find a strong, brave, manly kind of a man than in the military? What better place to see them in action than on deployment, where you might be more inclined to want a close relationship as you face IEDs and other hazards of deployment to a combat zone? This is not the time. These relationships can disrupt unit cohesion and result in poor decision making (for both of you). As you are well aware, women are a rare commodity in the war zone and on deployed ships. Your presence is known wherever you go. Heck, maybe you were one of only two or so women where you were. Dating and flirting in this atmosphere is problematic. You will become great, lifelong friends with the men you deploy with. Wait until you have returned from deployment and are back into the routine of your life before deciding to have a relationship with one of them.

Don't Be Too Hard on the Boys

Okay, so the reality is that women aren't treated equally in the military. Women can't hold some jobs, there are negative gender stereotypes to deal with, women are still facing dangers of sexual assault and sexual harassment, and women are held to a different standard. All of this complicates daily work, deployment, and postdeployment adjustment. But this is changing, and right now it is changing faster because of the wars in Afghanistan and Iraq. Women are proving themselves in very high-stress, dangerous situations. It is the continued exposure to successful military women that is going to normalize things for both military men and women. If the boys are acting badly, call them on it, but most of the time your actions will win the day. Represent women well.

Get Help If You Need It

One great difference between men and women is that women are more likely to ask for help (just as they are more likely to ask for directions when lost). Unfortunately, because of the increased scrutiny of women, some women are afraid of being seen as weak if they go get help.

This is just one of many reasons that service members don't seek care when they need it, and not just mental health care. Consider the case of the marine who went to jump school with a broken ankle so she wouldn't appear weak. You can probably guess how well that went. The point is that if you are having a hard time readjusting to noncombat life, you owe it to yourself to take action.

You've got several options here. First, if you are having serious symptoms that are affecting your ability to function, you need help, and you need it now. This help can be obtained at any military mental health clinic. If you are having thoughts of suicide (see Chapter 14), please seek assistance from a medical provider or your chain of command immediately. If your symptoms or concerns are not as serious or disturbing, you do have some options that will not be recorded in your medical record. Every branch of the military has counseling services (e.g., Navy Fleet and Family Services; see the Appendix for all of them) where you can go without a referral and nothing is put in your medical record. If the counselor who is seeing you doesn't think you have a serious problem such as PTSD or depression, he or she will see you confidentially. The chaplain is also always an option for you. Please note that most chaplains don't care what religion you are, or if you even believe in God. They are there to help everyone. The point is to see someone. If you let problems fester and don't do anything to help solve them, they only get worse. You as a service member deserve better than that—use the resources available to you.

A FEW FINAL THOUGHTS

The good news is that there are more women in the military than ever before and women are holding more jobs than ever before, to include being knowingly deployed into harm's way. The bad news is that women haven't yet reached a state of equality, and this extends all the way to the availability of female-specific postdeployment resources. More good news, however, is that you, as an individual military woman, are a part of getting military women there. You do have more hurdles than men, but these hurdles are gradually lessening as women are further integrated and accepted into the fold and more information is becoming available to mental health providers about the needs of female veterans and service members. But more bad news is that some of these hurdles are severe, like sexual assault and sexual harassment, which can make it impossible for you to do your job. In these cases, you must act. Go and get yourself help, and then work with your chain of command to take care of the problem at your command. Although the military isn't a perfect place for women yet, military leadership is taking strides to get there. There are resources for any problem you are facing as a result of deployment and to help make your military experience fulfilling, rewarding, and professionally challenging. Take advantage of them, and remember that military women have always been pioneers and role models for others. Never lose sight of the fact that you are making changes for other women, which makes you a part of something much bigger than yourself.

CHAPTER 8

IS MY SUBSTANCE USE OR GAMBLING OUT OF CONTROL?

Has someone told you that you need to cut down on your drinking? Or are you spending more money than ever on gambling? Maybe you have become addicted to pain medication. Maybe one of these things has increased since you got back from deployment. Maybe your spouse is reaching the end of his or her ability and willingness to cope with you because of one of these things. Maybe you have gotten yourself deep into debt. Or maybe you are simply curious to know whether how much you are drinking or gambling is normal. In this chapter, we address issues related to alcohol, drugs, and gambling and provide guidance as to what is considered normal and what might indicate a problem. We explain the military's policies on each and let you know where and how to get help if you need it. Please note that although this book is focused on problems after deployment, most of the information and guidelines here apply even if you haven't deployed.

Let's consider the case of SGT F., who deployed to Afghanistan a year ago. When he got to Afghanistan, he went through alcohol withdrawal symptoms for the first few days of the deployment. He thought about asking his wife to mail him alcohol, and he considered making his own or drinking mouthwash, but he ultimately decided to white knuckle his alcohol cravings during deployment. He didn't have too hard of a time doing this because the deployment was busy. When he got back, he started drinking again. He drank daily and rapidly increased how much he was drinking everyday. He and his wife started fighting about his alcohol use, something that they often did before the deployment, although his wife thought he was drinking more now and was also much more irritable and angry. One night after a fight, she began to fear for her safety and called his first sergeant. His command coordinated a room in the barracks and a referral to the army's alcohol program.

ALCOHOL

Before continuing with SGT F.'s case, let's discuss alcohol and those things that might indicate a problem. The military has a pretty solid relationship with alcohol. The military celebrates just about everything with it; personalized steins grace the clubs; port is a mandatory toast; hails and bails–farewells are not complete without alcohol; squadrons maintain their own bars; wetting downs revolve around alcohol as do most other initiations—you get the idea. A little known fact is that grog (that navy drink of rum or whiskey diluted with water) was the military's first substance abuse prevention effort, enacted by legislation in 1794. The rationale was to protect sailors by not giving them straight liquor. Although we aren't getting regular rations of alcohol anymore (we know—sometimes life isn't fair), alcohol is still a problem for the military, and maybe it is currently a problem for you or someone you care about. If you are concerned with your own or a friend's drinking, take a look at the questions here. If there are any yes answers, you might want to see someone or have a talk with the person you are concerned about (see more on that later).

- Does it take more drinks to get drunk than it used to?
- Have you hurt someone else while you were drinking, or have you been arrested because of your drinking?
- Do you continue to drink even though a doctor told you to stop?
- Do you continue to drink even though a family member or friend told you they think you are drinking too much?
- Have you had more than one alcohol-related blackout in your life? In other words, you don't remember what you did the night before (not the same as drinking until you pass out).
- Are you having problems at work because of your drinking?
- Do you drive after drinking even though you are buzzed or drunk?
- Do you drink every day?
- Are you finding yourself lying about your drinking?
- When you drink, do you routinely drink more than five drinks (for men; four drinks for women)? In other words, are you binge drinking?
- Is the only time you feel good when you are drinking?
- Have you tried to cut down or quit drinking but couldn't?
- Do you have physical symptoms when you stop drinking (e.g., shaking, sweating, feeling sick to your stomach)?
- Do you drink in the morning?
- Do you feel guilty about your drinking?
- Do you find yourself using alcohol to forget your worries or reduce anxiety or depression?

SGT F. has yes answers to many of these questions. He went through physical withdrawal symptoms in Afghanistan. His wife has told him she thinks he is drinking too much. He is drinking every day, and his tolerance has increased a lot. Because his wife has involved the command, he is now at risk of being in trouble at work. We return to SGT F. again in a minute, but let's first discuss the other addictions.

DRUG USE

Drug use is different from alcohol and gambling issues (see more about gambling in the next section) because it is usually illegal. Illegal drug use hasn't been too much of a problem for the military since the inception of the zero tolerance policy and continued mandatory command sweep and random drug screens for everyone. However, for a small percentage of service members, illegal drug use, abuse of prescription drugs, or abuse of substances never intended to be used to get high (e.g., huffing air freshener, computer cleaners, edge dressing) are a serious problem. And if you are abusing any of these substances even though you know it will get you fired and charged with a crime, you don't need to think too hard about it to know you have a drug problem. Getting help for a drug problem in the military can be challenging because as in the case of illicit drugs, you are highly likely to lose your job. Of course, continued use of the drug or drugs is likely to result in this anyway because it will only be a matter of time before you are caught by Operation Goldenflow or start messing up at work. Sometimes it is more important to put your health first, over your job. In the event that this is an issue for you, and even if you are getting processed for separation, the military will often give you treatment before discharging you if you want it.

Prescription medication abuse and substances that aren't illegal are a different story. If you have become addicted to pain medication, for example, after an injury or surgery, there are services that can be provided to you (detoxification and substance treatment if necessary), and a self-referral will probably not result in discharge from the military. Other forms of substance abuse and your military status will vary from command to command. Your commanding officer can discharge you from the military for any unauthorized use of a substance; however, we have seen many people get a second chance after an incident of this type. Usually, these are the people who admit that what they did was stupid, accept responsibility for their actions, and work hard to regain the trust of the command.

GAMBLING

It is estimated that of the approximately 2,200,000 active, reserve, and guard members, 1.2% have a gambling problem. This is a lot of people. A big problem with military gamblers is that of the service members seeking treatment at two military gambling treatment sites, 20% to 50% had seriously considered suicide or attempted suicide because of the problems that arose because of their gambling. The military views gambling as an addiction very much like alcoholism and drug dependence. The following questions[1] are provided by the Gamblers Anonymous website (http://www.gamblersanonymous.com) for individuals to determine whether they might have a gambling problem. Gamblers Anonymous guidance is that people with serious gambling problems will say yes to seven or more of the questions.

- Did you ever lose time from work or school because of gambling?
- Has gambling ever made your home life unhappy?
- Did gambling affect your reputation?
- Have you ever felt remorse after gambling?
- Did you ever gamble to get money with which to pay debts or otherwise solve financial difficulties?
- Did gambling cause a decrease in your ambition or efficiency?
- After losing, did you feel you must return as soon as possible and win back your losses?
- After a win, did you have a strong urge to return and win more?

---

[1]From *Twenty Questions* by Gamblers Anonymous. Available at http://www. gamblersanonymous.com. Reprinted with permission.

- Did you often gamble until your last dollar was gone?
- Did you ever borrow to finance your gambling?
- Have you ever sold anything to finance your gambling?
- Were you reluctant to use "gambling money" for normal expenditures?
- Did gambling make you careless of your welfare or that of your family?
- Did you ever gamble longer than you had planned?
- Have you ever gambled to escape worry, trouble, boredom, or loneliness?
- Have you ever committed, or considered committing, an illegal act to finance gambling?
- Did gambling cause you to have difficulty in sleeping?
- Do arguments, disappointments, or frustrations create within you an urge to gamble?
- Did you ever have an urge to celebrate any good fortune with a few hours of gambling?
- Have you ever considered self-destruction or suicide as a result of your gambling?

WHOM CAN I TALK TO?

Each branch of service has a formal substance program with appointed people at your command who can get you a referral for your drinking or other substance questions or problems. You can also talk to your doctor, a counselor, a mentor in your chain of command, or your chaplain. When you are ready, the military provides all levels of alcohol and drug rehabilitation (inpatient for detoxification, residential treatment, and two levels of outpatient treatment), depending on your needs. Gambling treatment is not as integrated, but a military mental health department can find you a treatment program. In the case of SGT F., he was referred through his command.

He met the criteria for alcohol dependence and received residential alcohol treatment.

Because SGT F. was not a self-referral, he did not have the following option. But you do if nothing has happened yet, so if you aren't ready to involve anyone in the military system but have decided you need help, you can also stop by an open Alcoholics Anonymous (AA), Narcotics Anonymous, or Gamblers Anonymous meeting. These meetings are free, and you don't need an appointment. In the case of AA, there are meetings continuously in every town in the United States, every U.S. military base around the world, and even many English-speaking meetings in other countries. At all of these meetings, the other members take your confidentiality very seriously (hence, the *anonymous* part of all of the names). These meetings do not replace treatment, but they are the means that most people in the military use to successfully remain alcohol, drug, or gambling free after treatment.

One thing about these meetings deserves mention. Sometimes people say that they don't want to go to AA, for instance, because of the emphasis on spirituality and God. We view this as an excuse not to get help with a problem. Many nonreligious and even atheist people with alcohol problems have been helped by AA. Some of them have even made up their own acronym, GoD (for Group of Drunks). In other words, put your trust in a "group of drunks" to help you with your own problem, which is exactly the basis for AA, Narcotics Anonymous, and Gamblers Anonymous; get support from people

Quick Fact

The military has a variety of treatment services to provide to you if you need help.

who truly understand what you are going through. If the hitch for you is the spiritual aspect of these meetings, get over it, as many people have done before you. To access one of these meetings, consult the white pages of the local phone book or find meetings by searching online (please see the Appendix for websites and other resources).

MY CAREER WILL BE AFFECTED IF I GET HELP FOR MY PROBLEM

Is this something to worry about? Well, of course. If you do have an addiction, getting treatment means that you leave work for 2 to 4 weeks and then have regular appointments afterward for a while. If your command isn't supportive, they may give you a hard time, and you might have to win back trust. Of course, the alternative is likely to be that you get worse, that you get in trouble, and then on top of needing treatment, you face legal action, financial distress, divorce, or disciplinary action at work. Careers aren't ruined because someone seeks alcohol or gambling treatment (however, this is not necessarily the case if you are using illicit drugs such as cocaine or methamphetamine). However, careers do end once someone has been arrested for driving under the influence or someone's work performance has suffered so much that he or she fails to promote. Once someone has been treated for an alcohol problem, for example, and is staying sober, it is routine for the military to continue maintenance of security clearances and special duties, such as flight status. You might be very surprised to know how many people have been successfully treated for their known drinking problem. Some of these are people you know and work with every day. Others hold high positions in the military or are flying high-performance tactical aircraft. Again, if you are successfully treated, your military career is not in jeopardy. It's when you let it go too far that you put your job at risk. Saving your career, health, and functioning of your family is worth the short-term discomfort.

Quick Fact

You are more likely to lose your career if you don't get help than you are by hiding problems.

SGT F. did not start off on the best foot. His first sergeant got a nighttime phone call from SGT F.'s wife, which is how the command learned of SGT F.'s problems with alcohol. However, even in this case SGT F.'s career is not over. SGT F. has been able to remain sober with the help of the military substance program and AA. He has been able to re-prove himself at work and has been able to maintain both his career and his security clearance. Because SGT F. had no disciplinary charges, his alcohol problem was treated as a medical problem that is now considered by his command to be treated. SGT F. needs to keep up his AA meetings to remain sober, but as far as his command is concerned, he is a full up round.

HOW DO I CONFRONT A FRIEND ABOUT HIS OR HER SUBSTANCE OR GAMBLING PROBLEM?

This is an extremely hard thing to do. Service members worry that their friends, who are also often their coworkers, will become angry if confronted. This might cause problems in the workplace and in their social lives. And you are right: Confronting someone about his or her drinking, gambling, drug use, or other behavior is hard and unpleasant. It is common for those being confronted not to take it well. If you truly have concerns about someone, however, you are dropping the ball by not saying something about it. One of the things most likely to clue someone in that they might have a problem is friends expressing concerns. Unfortunately, this usually takes some time to sink in. Not doing it, though, is the same as letting someone actively harm him- or herself. You owe it to a true friend to deal with your own discomfort and tell him or her what you have observed and what you think about it. Express concern and willingness to help your friend get help. Gambling deserves special note here. A lot of military gamblers in trouble have seriously considered or have attempted suicide. It is always a good idea to ask someone directly if they are thinking about hurting themselves. Many lives have been saved this way. Chapter 14 discusses how to do this.

SOMETIMES INCREASED ALCOHOL USE, DRUG USE, OR GAMBLING ARE WAYS TO HANDLE PROBLEMS RELATED TO DEPLOYMENT

As you probably know if you have taken an interest in this chapter, many people use alcohol as a way to relax, defuse after a stressful day, and, at times, cope with problems. Having a beer or two after work to unwind is fine, but if you find yourself having more drinks than usual or drinking more frequently to address significant problems, this may lead to serious trouble.

After deployment, service members often have to deal with unpleasant experiences they encountered on deployment, possibly the breakup of a relationship, other family problems they weren't expecting, or financial problems. You've probably already heard the term *self-medicate*, which is what some people try to do with alcohol, drugs, or gambling. These can all cover up unpleasant memories and emotions and allow a person to avoid feeling bad. The problem is that this does not allow the person to work through whatever he or she is dealing with. In fact, it prolongs the problem, which in turn makes it worse and harder for the person to eventually deal with whatever the issue is. Things can snowball, leading to further problems at home and at work and possibly even to legal charges if the drinking

> **Quick Fact**
>
> Use of alcohol, drugs, or gambling to cope with problems only makes the problems worse.

(fighting, driving drunk, public drunkenness, domestic violence, etc.), drug use (unsafe behavior, harm to self or others, arrest for drug activity, etc.), or gambling (loss of possessions, significant debt, illegal behavior to get money, etc.) gets out of control. Please also keep in mind that if you have been diagnosed with posttraumatic stress disorder, traumatic brain injury, or depression, you should stay away from alcohol so that you can recover.

A FEW FINAL THOUGHTS

Alcohol and drug use and gambling are common problems in general and are also ways in which some people try to handle the stress of deployment. They provide a temporary distraction, a means to avoid unpleasant symptoms and topics, and an escape to somewhere else. A little of this (e.g., an occasional night out with the boys or girls or a beer after work) is normal. However, for some people, this gets out of control. Fortunately, the military is highly motivated to help you manage any addiction problem and provides all levels of care. If you think you have a problem, talk to someone. You can speak with complete confidentiality to members of 12-step groups and to any military chaplain. When you are ready for help, the military will provide you an evaluation and get you the services you need.

CHAPTER 9

DEALING WITH THE GRIEF
OF LOSING A COMRADE

The military does a great job training its troops to win wars. You are taught proficiency in handling weapons, how to construct makeshift runways, life-saving emergency battlefield medical care, and how to make quick and effective decisions during times of immense emotional and physical stress. However, one area that is generally not covered during training is how to deal with the grief associated with losing a friend and colleague. And really, how could it be? Losing a comrade is one of the most difficult things any soldier, sailor, airman, or marine will ever have to go through. It is an event that all too many of you reading this book have experienced, and for most of you, it has permanently altered your life to some degree.

In addition to the sadness associated with losing a friend and fellow service member, you may be sidetracked by guilt, anger, remorse, or confusion. Questions such as "Why wasn't it me?" "Could I have done more?" "Is this my fault?" and "Why did our commander send us out on that mission?" may consume you. People cope with this experience in different ways. Some pick methods that are not the most effective. For example, some turn to alcohol or drugs as a way to cope with negative memories and feelings. Others become consumed with anger and resort to violence as a means of releasing

---

> **Quick Fact**
>
> Losing a friend is one of the toughest things for a service member to face.

---

pent-up hostility, and others withdraw from loved ones and sink into a deep depression. Regardless of how you react, the grief associated with losing a friend on the battlefield can be devastating.

The goals of this chapter are simple. First, we want you to be able to recognize grief in yourself and others. Second, we want you to know that grief is a normal reaction when a person loses someone they care about. And last, we provide you with tips on how to manage grief after losing a fellow service member.

WHAT IS GRIEF?

In the simplest terms, *grief* is the emotional reaction a person has to a loss. Grief can take many forms and can be associated with physical, behavioral, interpersonal, and philosophical challenges. The type of loss can vary and range from the loss of a job to the death of a spouse or parent. The level of grief an individual experiences after a loss depends on such things as the emotional connection to the person or thing that was lost, the length of time since the loss, and the level of support and comfort available from loved ones. In most cases, grief is a normal reaction. However, in some cases it can become complicated and turn into something more serious.

Because loss is a common human experience, everyone will experience grief. It's not a matter of if, but of when and to what degree. Grief is categorized as either normal or complicated. During episodes of normal grief, most people experience periods of sadness, sorrow, guilt, anger, and emotional numbness. However, over time the intensity of these feelings fades as the person comes to terms with the loss. For some service members, the normal grief reaction does not diminish gradually over time but instead becomes a very painful, ongoing experience. This is called *complicated grief*. In complicated grief, the person is not fully able to put the loss behind him or her and continues to suffer. Please remember that everyone is different and won't experience complicated grief in the same way, but generally symptoms of complicated grief include

- continued focus on the loss and memories of the loved one,
- inability to accept the death of the loved one,
- extreme longing for the loved one,
- emotional numbness,
- uncontrollable crying spells,
- inability to experience pleasure in life,
- prolonged sadness,
- recurrent emotionally charged dreams about the loved one,
- difficulty carrying out normal daily routines (e.g., cleaning, cooking, paying bills),
- withdrawing from friends and family,
- difficulty forming new close relationships,
- anger or extreme irritability, and
- lack of trust in others.

As a general rule, "normal" grief typically lasts from 3 to 6 months. However, this is highly variable and depends on the person's culture, connection with the loved one, and available social support. Complicated grief can continue for years. Also, during the initial months the symptoms of normal and complicated grief are the same. But remember, as we mentioned earlier, people react differently to loss. In some cultures and religions, grief that lasts only a few weeks or that lasts to some degree for many years may be considered normal. Not everybody wears a size nine combat boot.

> **Quick Fact**
>
> Not everyone handles losing a friend the same way.

DEALING WITH GRIEF

Grief hurts, and many people try to avoid these feelings by ignoring them and hoping they'll go away. It doesn't work like that. Trying to ignore grief will actually make it worse and last longer. Others think that the best thing you can do is to be tough and seem unaffected when confronted with the death of a friend. Sometimes being tough for the other service members who are also dealing with the same death means that you aren't afraid to show them that you are hurting, too. No one expects you to be unfazed by a death. Showing your genuine feelings is a good thing.

A misconception about grief is that crying is a requirement. It is true that many people, both men and women, cry when they are upset. But some people express their feelings in other ways, so there is no mandatory crying in grief. By far the biggest concern about coping with a death is the notion that if you move on with your life, you are somehow forgetting the person you lost. Moving forward is not a selfish act. It is what you have to do for yourself and all of the other people in your life. Trust us, you will never forget your friend, and he or she wouldn't want you to feel horrible forever.

Here are a few things you can do to help yourself deal with the grief.

Get Support

When experiencing grief, it is important to surround yourself with people you care about and who care about you. Family and friends are the best source of support during difficult times. Talk with a chaplain or other service members who know what it's like to lose someone on the battlefield.

Express Your Feelings

Part of the grieving process is verbalizing your feelings about the death. Talk with someone you trust about your sadness, anger, or confusion. If it's difficult for you to talk about your feelings, write them down instead.

Be Patient

Remind yourself that the grieving process is not a quick one. It can take many months for things to get back to normal. Don't rush things. Allow yourself time to grieve.

Stay Active

Don't spend your weekends sitting at home thinking about the loss. Continue on with your life. Go out with friends, visit with family, and have fun. Remembering the person is a healthy part of the grieving process, but be careful not to let your life become consumed by it.

Take Care of Your Physical Needs

It's critical that you get enough sleep and eat and exercise regularly. Poor nutrition and sleep deprivation only aggravate grief.

Quick Fact
You can't rush the grieving process.

Avoid Alcohol and Drugs

Self-medicating your negative feelings is a surefire way to make things worse. Instead of drowning or suppressing your feelings with alcohol or drugs, talk with someone about how you're feeling.

Read a Book on Death and Grief

Reading books about overcoming the death of a loved one is a great way to get better. Good examples are *When Will I Stop Hurting? Dealing With a Recent Death* by June Cerza Kolf and *I Wasn't Ready to Say Goodbye: Surviving, Coping and Healing After the Sudden Death of a Loved One* by Brook Noel.

Develop a Memorial

Creating a memorial to your friend is a great way to deal with any unresolved feelings of grief you may have. In our experience working with service members, creating a plaque, drawing, painting, or getting a tattoo can bring relief.

Join a Support Group

Sharing your experiences with others who have experienced the death of a loved one can be very helpful. If you aren't ready to meet with others in person or there isn't a group available, consider joining an online support group that deals with grief. One example is http://www.griefnet.org.

A FEW FINAL THOUGHTS

Losing a friend and colleague is a very difficult experience that many service members are required to face. As military psychologists, we have seen the toughest of the tough brought to their knees by the immense grief that accompanies this inevitable and distressing consequence of war. In getting through this difficult process, it's important to remember that many before you have walked in your boots and know how difficult it is to lose a friend. It's also important to know that most have made it through with the help of family, friends, and fellow service members. Don't swallow your feelings. Deal with this problem promptly and effectively. You have a responsibility to yourself, your family, your country, and your fallen friend to move forward with your life.

CHAPTER 10

LIVING WITH TAKING ANOTHER'S LIFE

Taking the life of another human being is something that every service member is potentially faced with during his or her military career, but it becomes more of a likelihood when you get deployed to a combat zone. In the past, troops serving in support roles were less likely to face this horrific task of war when compared with those on the frontlines. Today, however, frontlines have blurred, and the battlefields have given way to 360° perimeters that need defending at all times. Consequently, anyone at anytime may be called on to act as an infantryman, rifleman, or cavalry scout.

If you used only television and movies to know what it is like to kill another person, you would have an extremely unrealistic view of the act. The popular media portray the act of taking another human's life as being as easy as snuffing out a cigarette in an ashtray. Those of you who have had to kill know it is not that simple. Among military personnel who have taken a life, most have varying degrees of guilt, shame, grief, sadness, and remorse and various ethical, moral, and religious concerns about killing. These feelings can be present even if the person was trying to kill you at the time! Those of you who made a conscious decision not to kill may also be experiencing the same emotions. If you use your training and make a conscious decision to

---

> **Quick Fact**
>
> Anyone may be required to kill in combat at any time.

kill the enemy, then you will be faced with the guilt that you decided to kill someone else. However, if you decide not to kill, then you might have to deal with the guilt of not using your training as a warfighter. Either way, the psychological consequences can be very hard to deal with.

The emotional consequences that often accompany the act of taking the life of another person are intense and difficult to address. Therefore, in this chapter it is our intent to help you understand the emotional and psychological consequences of taking another human's life and how to overcome any problems that may arise.

THE EMOTIONAL STAGES OF KILLING

In *On Killing,* Lt. Col. Dave Grossman talks about the different emotional stages that service members go through after they have killed. On the basis of countless interviews with combat veterans, he broke down the psychological process of killing into five stages: *concern, killing, exhilaration, remorse,* and *rationalization and acceptance.*

The concern stage takes place before having to kill. The service member begins to question himself as to whether he can pull the trig-

---

> **Quick Fact**
>
> Guilt, shame, and remorse can result from deciding to kill an enemy and from deciding not to kill an enemy in a combat zone.

ger. Questions such as "Will I freeze?" or "Do I have what it takes?" begin to surface. The killing stage covers the actual act of killing. For most service members, it is automatic and rooted in the countless hours spent practicing at the firing range: two quick shots at center mass. Typically, it happens without thinking. If the service member is unable to pull the trigger, then guilt and shame may emerge from this inability to act. The third stage, exhilaration, describes the intense satisfaction and contentment that can follow. Although the average nonmilitary person may find it unfathomable that another human would derive satisfaction from taking another's life, this is not an uncommon reaction for combat troops. However, it has less to do with the actual killing and more to do with the satisfaction of fulfilling the role of a good warrior and being successful at one's job. Immediately after this exhilaration, the service member may experience the emotional fallout of the remorse stage. During this stage, the individual may experience tremendous guilt and self-loathing. If these emotions go unresolved, the person may spend decades fixated on the act, which can lead to alcohol and drug use, depression, and various other problems. The final stage, rationalization and acceptance, can be a lifelong process in which the service member attempts to come to terms with having had to kill. For some, this happens while still in theater. For others, it may only come after years of reflection and self-understanding.

It is important to note that not all people negotiate these stages in the same way. Some may experience greater or lesser degrees of distress than others. What is universal, however, is that the act of killing is not without emotional consequences. It is just a matter of degree.

Quick Fact

Killing is not without emotional consequences.

SETTING UP PSYCHOLOGICAL PERIMETERS

Just as people respond differently to the act of killing, people also vary in how they handle or cope with it. For most, psychological defense mechanisms come into play. *Defense mechanisms* are ways people protect themselves from unpleasant thoughts, feelings, and behaviors. Think of them as a kind of emotional body armor, although some strategies are better to use than others. They are often unconscious and range from things like denial (refusal to accept reality) to acting out (getting into a fight instead of recognizing that you are angry and upset and dealing with it). An example of a more effective defense mechanism is *compensation*—the ability to balance both positive and negative aspects of a situation.

Service members who have killed on the battlefield engage in several consistent defense mechanisms that are effective and adaptive. The most common one is *rationalization*. Rationalization is used by intelligent people and involves looking at something in a different light or coming up with an explanation for one's perceptions or behaviors when faced with a difficult reality. For example, a marine fresh out of boot camp kills an enemy during a firefight in Afghanistan. As a way to combat the negative feelings this event caused, he tells himself that the enemy was trying to kill his fire team and that if he hadn't killed the Afghan, he would have killed both the marine and the other members of his team. This rationalization allows the marine to view his actions as necessary when compared with the alternatives.

Another common defense mechanism service members use is *suppression*, the conscious decision to not pay attention to an emotion or need to cope with the current reality. For instance, a seasoned Air Force medic has learned to block out all the death and dismemberment she has witnessed on the battlefield. Through suppression, the medic has learned how to function well in her job despite the horri-

Quick Fact
Rationalization and suppression are adaptive defense mechanisms that help service members deal with killing.

ble things she has witnessed. However, this is typically only effective for the short term, and the memories will need to be dealt with at some point.

Another variable that influences the degree to which the service member will be affected by killing has to do with his or her physical, emotional, or psychological distance from the person who is killed. Physical distance is directly related to emotional or psychological distance. For example, a fighter pilot who destroys a house full of insurgents from the air will likely feel less emotional distress than the marine who is forced to kill an enemy combatant up close with a knife. In the latter instance, the killing is much more personal and the marine is more likely to struggle with the emotional consequences of the act. Increased physical distance helps the service member separate him- or herself from the enemy, whereas decreased physical distance does just the opposite. If your situation was very up close and personal, it is natural to have strong emotions tied to those actions.

GUILT, SHAME, AND DEPRESSION

We have already mentioned that killing another human can bring about shame and guilt. However, killing can cause many other negative emotions. For example, all of you have experienced shame and guilt to some extent at some point in your lives. Maybe you lied to your spouse about how much money you spent at the mall or misled your first sergeant about how far you traveled from base without the proper pass. Shame and guilt are part of the human experience. Some experts believe that these troubling emotions are healthy in that they can help keep us in check and prevent us from engaging in socially inappropriate behavior. It's when the guilt and shame become pervasive and dominate the individual's thoughts that these emotions can lead to depression.

As psychologists, we are well aware of how shame and guilt go hand in hand with depression. Individuals become withdrawn, and their social supports consequently wither away. Without family, friends, and fellow combat veterans to provide support and understanding, the individual can become hopeless and apathetic about life. He or she may develop negative thinking patterns and may only be able to focus on what goes wrong in his or her life. Think of the classic story of the person who wins the lottery, but all he can do is complain about all the taxes he has to pay on his winnings. Some may turn to alcohol, drugs, or both to deal with the pain in an attempt to quiet their mind. As you might expect, this can lead to many additional problems, such as further isolation from friends and families, as well as work, legal, and health problems. In some extreme and tragic cases, suicide feels like the only way out. An already vulnerable person may only need one more stressful event to push him or her over the edge. If you are experiencing suicidal thoughts, you should immediately go to someone within your chain of command whom you trust. If there is no one there, go to a friend, family member, or military chaplain. If you can't find anyone, go to the emergency room at your local base or post.

Quick Fact

Shame and guilt go hand in hand with depression.

HOW TO OVERCOME THE GUILT OF KILLING

Dealing with the guilt over killing can be a challenge for the most seasoned service member, but it can be managed with some time and effort. Here are a few things you can do.

Acknowledge the Guilt and Shame

As with any problem, the first step is to acknowledge that there is a problem. The harder you try to avoid the shame and guilt associated with killing, the longer it will take you to get over it. It's important to realize that what you are going through is what most service members in your situation have gone through. You are not broken, crazy, or any less of a warrior for feeling the way you do.

Challenge Any Negative Beliefs You Have About Killing During War

If you have read other chapters in this book, it will be no surprise to you that how a person interprets an event has an impact on how he or she will feel and behave. Maintaining negative perceptions about the event only fuels the shame and guilt. Don't be afraid to challenge and replace negative beliefs such as "I'm a killer/murderer," "God will never forgive me," or "Something bad will happen to me because of what I did." Instead, make statements such as "I was doing my job," "He would have killed me," or "I was able to save others."

Talk With Another Service Member or Veteran Who Has Also Experienced Killing

There is no better person to help you put this into perspective than another service member or veteran who has also killed. Ask them how they got through it. Tell them how you feel and how it has altered your life. Allow them to help normalize this event for you. Remember, you are not the first person who has taken a life in combat. Thousands before you have had to deal with this. Accept that it is part of war, and move forward.

Talk With a Chaplain, Minister, Priest, or Other Spiritual Leader

Taking a life has profound religious and moral implications for many service members. Rely on your unit chaplain or personal spiritual leader to help you navigate this difficult issue. Spiritual leaders have a knack for helping people come to grips with difficult moral, spiritual, and religious conflicts. You could say that they are the subject-matter experts in this area.

Read *On Killing: The Psychological Cost of Learning to Kill in War and Society*

This book is a must-read for anyone who has been forced to take another's life in combat. It covers nearly every aspect of killing and provides insight into how killing affects the warrior. You will be surprised at how many stories of the men in this book you will be able to relate to.

Seek Professional Help

As always, seek help if you are not able to manage things on your own or with the help of a friend or family member. The military has

---

Quick Fact

Talking with your chaplain, minister, priest, or other spiritual leader can help.

psychologists, psychiatrists, counselors, and social workers for a reason. Use them!

A FEW FINAL THOUGHTS

In the movie *Unforgiven,* Clint Eastwood said, "It's a hell of a thing, killin' a man, you take away all he's got and all he's ever gonna have." His statement is a testament to the fact that killing is not as simple as snuffing out a cigarette. It is an act that only a relatively few people will experience in their lifetime. It is riddled with many emotions and has the potential to alter a person's life forever. Remember, you are a warrior. You are trained to defend your country and have made a pledge to do everything in your power to see that the rest of us are safe. Acknowledge what happened, be proud that you did your job, and sleep well knowing that a nation is grateful for your sacrifices.

CHAPTER 11

DUCKING UNDER THE TABLE: LEARNING TO LIVE WITH HYPERSTARTLE

Most of you are familiar with the television and movie portrayals of the Vietnam era veteran who while walking down the street hits the ground or ducks behind a bush after a car backfires. Nonmilitary onlookers might be shown cautiously laughing, staring in confusion, or using disparaging remarks like "he's crazy," "shell shocked," or "fried" as they walk away in the opposite direction. Yet combat veterans in the know realize that a defensive reaction can be perfectly normal, particularly right after you get back. Take SGT J., for example.

SGT J. returned from a 12-month deployment to Afghanistan 1 month ago. Ever since he's been back, he's noticed that he jumps at every little noise. For example, last weekend while he and his wife were walking through the mall, a child accidentally popped the balloon she was carrying. SGT J. jumped and turned to see where the noise was coming from. It felt like his heart was about to jump out of his chest, and he felt his hands shaking. SGT J. was relieved once he realized what had happened. He also felt a little embarrassed by his reaction.

In this chapter, it is our intent to shed some light on this behavior, *hyperstartle,* that often follows those from the combat zone home. In doing this, we explain in more detail what hyperstartle is and what causes it. We also provide you with some tips on how to manage it so you don't become that guy who heads under the desk every time the first sergeant slams his door.

THINGS CAN BE A LITTLE MORE SERIOUS

Sometimes responses like those of SGT J. can be a symptom of something more serious, such as posttraumatic stress disorder, more commonly referred to as PTSD. The next chapter in this book describes PTSD in more detail, but it is appropriate at this point to mention that PTSD is a serious problem, and military and civilian experts have estimated that thousands of combat veterans are currently experiencing it. PTSD is caused by exposure to a traumatic experience such as witnessing a friend die or being personally faced with a near-death event. It consists of many symptoms, including flashbacks (i.e., reliving the traumatic experience); avoidance of people, activities, or thoughts about the traumatic event; sleep problems; and hyperstartle. It is *hyperstartle,* or being easily startled by loud noises, that we focus on in this chapter.

It is of the utmost importance for you to understand that being startled by loud noises does not mean you have PTSD. It means that you have one symptom of the disorder but not necessarily the disorder itself. You wouldn't say that someone has pneumonia just because they have a cough or a brain tumor because they complain of a headache. All too often, people incorrectly assume that just because someone has hyperstartle then they must also have PTSD. This is not the case.

Quick Fact

Being startled by loud noises does not mean you have PTSD.

HYPERSTARTLE: WHY DOES IT HAPPEN?

Many mental health professionals attempt to understand these kinds of things through a three-pronged approach: biological, psychological, and social, or *biopsychosocial* for short. For example, scientists know that the brain changes after exposure to a frightening event. Much of this is the result of chemical changes in the brain (some of them biological). Experts also know that how people are brought up affects how they handle and adapt to stress later in life. So, the social aspects of a person's life (e.g., one's relationship with one's parents or previous exposure to traumatic events) help determine how he or she will respond to future challenges. The psychological realm—how people tend to view or interpret events—is also crucial, in that thinking influences behavior. As you can see, many factors are involved in creating and maintaining psychological symptoms. However, there is another approach to understanding how these things develop, which is not completely unrelated to the biopsychosocial approach. It is called *classical conditioning.*

Classical conditioning is the cornerstone of behavioral psychology. It is a type of associative learning that was introduced by Ivan Pavlov. Some of you may remember him from high school or college (you know, Pavlov's dogs?). He became famous for pointing out that when you ring a bell right before you feed a dog, the dog will salivate when he hears the bell even in the absence of the food. In other words, the dog learns to associate the bell with the food and thinks he is about to be fed. This is sort of what happens with hyperstartle. You have been conditioned so that every time you hear a loud noise, your brain and body are saying to you, "Hey, the last time we heard something like this was in Iraq right after a mortar landed 200 meters from us. Hit the deck!" Although this is a very simple explanation of how you interpret things, classical conditioning best fits with what we know about the continued response to loud noises after returning from combat.

> **Quick Fact**
>
> Hyperstartle is the body's and mind's way of protecting you from harm.

Another important point is that hyperstartle often goes hand in hand with hypervigilance. *Hypervigilance* is basically being on guard all of the time. In the combat environment, your brain helps you maintain a keen awareness of your surroundings. This awareness helps protect you by warning you of impending danger so that your hyperstartle response can happen, helping you duck a little faster and miss that shrapnel or bullet that comes whizzing by your head. So in a combat environment, this is very adaptive. It's when it continues after you return home that it becomes a problem.

TURNING DOWN THE NOISE

So far we have talked about what causes hyperstartle and how it is a common occurrence in service members returning from deployment. We have also reviewed how hyperstartle is not the same thing as PTSD. In this section, we review a few things you can do to put this behind you.

Remind Yourself That It's Normal

Keep in mind that this is a problem that happens to many service members after deployment. Remind yourself that it doesn't mean you are crazy, fried, burned out, or anything similar. If it helps, talk to your fellow service members about it. It's likely that you will find that most of them have experienced or are experiencing hyperstartle to some degree.

Wait

Give it some time. It can take months for your mind and body to adjust after returning from deployment. Many problems such as insomnia, hypervigilance, and hyperstartle will correct themselves given enough time. Be patient and focus on your family, friends, and those things in your life that you enjoy.

Extinguish the Response

Because hyperstartle is a conditioned response, you can try to "uncondition" it. Have one of your buddies slam a door for 15 minutes straight so that your brain and body can learn that loud noises don't always mean danger is on its way. Go see a fireworks display. This may seem a bit silly, but it does work. However, keep in mind that if the noises become too distressing, you will need to stop. It is possible that you may need to seek the services of a professional.

Learn to Relax

Train your body to function at a lower level of stress through deep breathing, progressive muscle relaxation (tensing and relaxing your muscles), and visualization (go to your happy place). Use this as an excuse to get a massage or spend time in a hot tub. Being stressed out and on edge all of the time can make you jumpier. The more stressed you are, the more you will easily startled. So, learn and use proven ways to relax.

Quick Fact

The passing of time and learning to relax will help your body and mind reset itself.

Get More Sleep

You are likely aware of the fact that you are more easily agitated and have a shorter temper when you don't get enough sleep. This puts you on edge, which increases your chances of becoming easily startled or shaken. If you are having sleep difficulty, please see Chapter 3.

Laugh at Yourself

It's always important to not take yourself so seriously. Humor is a great way to overcome the physiological excitement your body goes through after being startled.

Seek the Help of a Professional

As noted earlier in the chapter, hyperstartle can be a sign of a more serious problem. If you notice a negative change in your mood, work performance, or home life, or if you develop any other symptoms such as nightmares, flashbacks, or insomnia, read the next chapter to see whether PTSD might be an issue for you.

A FEW FINAL THOUGHTS

Making the transition from combat zone to home can be challenging for many reasons. Common but troubling problems such as hyper-startle can stress you unnecessarily. The tips provided here will help you overcome this issue so that you can continue to move forward with life. Please keep in mind that if you notice that your problems are becoming more severe or that you are engaging in behaviors that aren't good for you, such as drinking more to be able to relax, it is important to get help from a professional. You don't have to deal with this on your own.

CHAPTER 12

WHAT IS PTSD, DO I HAVE IT, AND WHAT CAN I DO ABOUT IT?

Remember when you were getting ready to end deployment and you got that screening about disturbing dreams and memories, feeling disconnected from others, reexperiencing traumatic situations, and the like? If you were like everyone else, you checked "no, no, no, I'm not experiencing any of that" on your deployment health assessment. Sleep was great. Mood was great. No physical problems. Just get me the heck out of here. Well, maybe sleep wasn't great, and you were having disturbing dreams. Maybe a persistent sense of vague dread hung around you, or you just didn't feel yourself. Maybe you didn't feel connected to your family or community anymore.

Every person is affected by deployment. This might be short term as you transition back into your family and your predeployment routine. This might be long term as you cope with a loss of fellow service members killed in combat, learn to live with a serious injury and loss of physical functioning, or struggle with something you did or saw during the deployment. Like we said, people are changed by deployments.

Don't get us wrong, this isn't necessarily a bad thing. Everyone grows from new experiences, and there are obviously a lot of new experiences to be had when in foreign countries on deployment. You

> **Quick Fact**
>
> It is normal to feel different after deployment.

face difficult decisions; you deal with loneliness and frustration but also feelings of accomplishment; you get bored and figure out new ways to keep yourself occupied; you learn new ways to deal with stress; you get older; you make lifelong friends. In the deployed environment, you change, adapt, and grow, and often you have to deal with extraordinary stressors.

WHAT ABOUT WHEN I FEEL SO DIFFERENT THAT I THINK SOMETHING IS WRONG?

As we noted, deployment experiences, particularly to a combat zone, can result in a variety of changes to you emotionally. Some of these changes are negative and unpleasant. Many people don't want to hear that. Military members pride themselves on their inner strength in the face of war and adversity. The reality, however, is that deployments, combat situations, training accidents when people are hurt or killed, and other mishaps can affect us in ways that we don't expect and that we don't like. One of these ways is post-traumatic stress disorder, or PTSD—and PTSD has been in the news a lot lately.

One thing you need to know about PTSD is that some of its symptoms are normal. After a traumatic event, sleep can be disrupted and you might not be very trusting. Maybe you are more on guard and are avoiding things that remind you of the experience. As the previous chapter explains, maybe loud noises make you want to dive for cover. However, for a lot of people these things wear off as they confide in their friends and family, talk to other service members

---

Quick Fact
PTSD is your brain's way of protecting you.

with similar experiences, and just generally take care of themselves. So just because you can relate to some of the stuff you are about to read, this doesn't mean you have PTSD. But if these symptoms are so strong that you can't function as well as you used to or they won't go away, maybe you do, so read on and decide the best course of action for yourself.

PTSD can develop after someone experiences a significant personal trauma. This might be a car accident, a rape, a near-death experience, an aviation mishap, or, of course, combat. Combat in particular provides many opportunities for PTSD to develop. When a traumatizing event occurs, your body and brain try to protect you from the experience. Maybe your brain will try to make you forget things and try to lock them away. Maybe your body gets hyperalert and jumpy in certain environments or when you hear certain sounds or smell certain smells, even when you aren't in the combat zone anymore. When this gets out of control, we call it *PTSD*.

SYMPTOMS OF PTSD

This chapter is not meant to diagnose you. It is intended to let you know what PTSD is and to give you some information so that you can decide whether seeing someone might help you. Also, PTSD affects people differently, even if they developed it in response to the exact same event, so please keep in mind that the list of symptoms you are about to read will vary from person to person.

To get a diagnosis of PTSD, you have to have experienced a traumatic event in which you or someone near you died or was seriously injured or was at serious risk of dying or being gravely injured. After this kind of event, we try to figure out how to cope. We try to integrate what happened into what we know about ourselves. And, as noted earlier, our brain and body try to protect us from the discomfort and make us extra alert to future danger. When PTSD has developed, the symptoms can include

- disturbing memories of the event;
- nightmares;
- feeling like the event is happening again;
- avoiding things and people that remind you of the event;
- trying not to think or talk about what happened;
- memory loss for the event;
- feeling disconnected from others;
- feeling like your future has been cut short;
- sleep problems;
- irritability, temper problems, or both;
- problems concentrating;
- being startled easily (hyperstartle); and
- being excessively watchful for danger.

WHAT DOES PTSD LOOK LIKE?

PTSD is a personally unique experience. Everyone who ends up developing it doesn't have exactly the same symptoms, and those who have similar symptoms don't have them at the same rate. Here are some examples to help give a picture of what it might look like.

PFC A. found himself in a combat zone shortly out of boot camp at the age of 19. Not long into his deployment, while on a routine patrol, his squad came under surprise attack. He returned fire, killing many of the enemy, and was credited for saving much of his unit. He was awarded the Bronze Star. However, although many described his actions to him, PFC A. had no memory of the event. After returning from deployment, he began to be excessively fearful and was constantly on edge. He would patrol the grounds around the barracks at night and refused to sleep in his rack, preferring the floor. He developed insomnia and extreme irritability and several times physically attacked friends who accidentally surprised him, choking one until he left bruises on his throat. Afterward, he was tearful and told a friend he felt like he might be losing his mind.

SGT B. deployed to Iraq early in the war. Although he was working a checkpoint, a roadside bomb detonated, injuring SGT B.'s leg and fatally wounding several Iraqi children who were playing nearby. When he was taken to the hospital, the children had already been rushed in, and medical personnel were frantically trying to save their lives. He was overwhelmed by the sights, sounds, and especially the smells. He was unable to get the images of the dying children out of his mind. He was flown to Germany and then to the States for further care, where he recovered fully from the injury to his leg. Despite this, he started drinking heavily to try and numb his anxiety and get rid of his disturbing memories.

HM3 C. deployed to Afghanistan as an X-ray technician. A chief in her chain of command began to express a romantic interest in her, scheduling his shifts to be working when she was and following her to chow. She was unsure how to tell him she was not interested because she was concerned that he had authority over her. One night while they both were working an overnight shift, he cornered her and raped her. She felt extreme shame and embarrassment about this and fear of what his fellow chiefs would do to her if she reported him. As the deployment progressed, she became withdrawn, fearful of being alone, unable to sleep, often felt as though the rape was happening again and was unable to concentrate on her job. She was eventually removed from her duties for making mistakes, yet she did not report the rape.

> **Quick Fact**
>
> Anyone can develop PTSD, and PTSD is not a sign of weakness.

Cpt. D. was the copilot of a helicopter tasked with picking up some marines who were taking fire and suffering casualties. When he arrived at the landing zone, marines appeared, carrying the wounded and killed. Cpt. D. jumped out to help and began loading in wounded marines while taking fire. Cpt. D. picked up what ended up being just the torso of a marine killed in action, while someone else began picking up the other remaining body parts and handing them in to Cpt. D. While taking off, they were fired on by a rocket-propelled grenade that almost caused a crash. Cpt. D. had been fired on multiple times in combat, and although he experienced an adrenaline rush each time, he had not experienced any other problems. However, after this event he became overly cautious in the helicopter, experienced intrusive thoughts of the marine whose body was in pieces, became convinced he would die at any moment, and began avoiding combat missions.

DO I HAVE PTSD?

You should always be careful about trying to diagnose yourself. Our best advice to you here is that if you are bothered by any of the symptoms noted here or your spouse, significant other, or a family member is telling you that they are concerned about you because they think you have some of those symptoms (even if you think they are wrong), you should see someone. If you find yourself drinking more, starting to gamble, or using medications or drugs more frequently, or you don't feel like you are functioning like you used to, we would recommend that you get checked out.

> **Quick Fact**
>
> If you are concerned you might have PTSD, the best thing to do is to get it checked out.

Maybe you don't want to go directly to the mental health department. That's normal, and for some people going to see the shrink may not be necessary. If you don't want to make an appointment with a psychologist or psychiatrist, you can also first go to see a chaplain or counselor who can help you figure out whether it might be good for you to see a doctor. The important thing is that you go talk to an objective person who can help you decide.

HOW IS PTSD TREATED?

The good news is that PTSD can be successfully treated. We won't lie to you, though. It's hard work. Some PTSD treatment might involve medications, like sleeping aids. You will need to make a decision about taking medications by meeting with a psychiatrist or psychologist who prescribes medications. However, most people need talk therapy either by itself or in conjunction with medications to get better.

There are a couple of different kinds of therapy that research has shown work well, and these forms of therapy rely on the same two core principles of treatment: (a) You have to reexperience the event (we know that doesn't sound good, but keep reading), and (b) you have to learn to think about the event in a different way. During therapy, you are guided through the event in your mind so that you experience it all over again. This part of PTSD treatment sometimes makes people not want to get treatment because it makes them very uncomfortable, and they don't want to experience the event again by talking or thinking about it. By reexperiencing it, though, you can learn how to stop what are called *reexperiencing symptoms,* like the nightmares and feeling as though the event is happening again. Like an infected wound, the only way to stop the infection is to open it up and clean it out.

The other thing that happens in therapy is that you will teach your brain, which thinks it is helping you by doing things like avoiding the topic and trying not to remember, to think about the event in a different way. A person in treatment for PTSD learns how to look at the event differently and in a way that doesn't result in the very unpleasant symptoms that come with PTSD. You get to gain the upper hand on the event and start to control how you think about it instead of letting it keep control of some of your feelings, behaviors, and decisions.

Group therapy for PTSD can also be very helpful because not only can other people provide support, but they can also help you learn to work through what happened to you so that you can get on with your life. Military members who have PTSD because of combat experiences find a lot of support and kinship in groups of fellow warriors. Some people say they don't want to go to group therapy because they don't want to look weak or tell personal information to a bunch of other people. But most people, after they have gone to a group meeting or two, feel relief from their symptoms because they connect with people who are also military, have similar symptoms, and have had a lot of the same experiences. We recommend that if your doctor says group therapy would be good for you, you give it a try.

Going to see a doctor or other therapist for help with PTSD isn't the same as going to the doctor for a cold. If you just need a pill, you don't have to talk much to the doctor and you don't even really need to like him or her. But for therapy, you have to form a good relationship with the therapist. You have to feel comfortable asking the therapist questions about the treatment, your symptoms, and

Quick Fact

PTSD treatment is hard work, but it works.

anything that you may experience outside of the therapy sessions. You also have to understand that, just as in a hard workout where you sometimes need some outside motivation to perform your best ("My grandmother can do more pushups than you!" "You call that a pull-up?!"), your therapist is going to push you to do some things you may not really want to do or even believe that maybe you can't do. But just like working out where your run gets faster, you do more pushups or pull-ups, and you become bigger (or smaller, depending on your goals) and more toned, the temporary discomfort is worth it. And just like working out extends your life, lowers your stress levels, and makes you look and feel better, so will your treatment for PTSD.

A FEW FINAL THOUGHTS

Not everyone who experiences a traumatic event gets PTSD, and PTSD isn't the only thing that can happen when something really bad happens to you. On the plus side, after experiencing something horrible, you will probably learn to cope in new ways, and you may become even more resilient to stress for future deployments. Unfortunately, other things can happen. Some of these are temporary and go away on their own, like a short period of sadness or hyper-startle, and others are very serious and require professional help, such as major depression or the development of a phobia.

PTSD is thought of as a problem common to warriors because the combat zone is ripe for traumatic experiences. PTSD, and other serious problems that arise during combat or other trauma, can also affect anyone—enlisted, officers, men, women, young, not so young, you name it. Duty in the current deployed environments is dangerous, and all are at risk of developing problems, not the least of which is PTSD. The good news is that the military takes PTSD seriously, and there are good options for treatment. If you think you might have it or you know for sure that you do, go and see someone.

CHAPTER 13

WHAT'S ALL OF THIS TALK ABOUT MILD TRAUMATIC BRAIN INJURY?

There has been a lot in the news lately about how many people are experiencing concussions or mild traumatic brain injuries in the Iraq and Afghanistan wars. One thing that is confusing about these terms is that they actually mean the same thing. We like to use the word *concussion* because most people already understand what it means, and people know a lot about concussions because of sports. Football players, boxers, hockey players, rugby players, and the like get concussions all of the time. The odds are that you may have had a concussion before you came into the military while playing sports in high school or college or doing something else (some of our favorites: jumping off of a building duct-taped between two mattresses and skateboard–skiing behind a truck at a high speed—you get the idea). A lot of people in the war have been diagnosed with a concussion, and some people seem to have a harder time getting better than others. In this chapter, we explain what a concussion is, what usually happens after a concussion, what might complicate recovery, and what you can do.

WHAT EXACTLY IS A CONCUSSION?

A concussion is a mild brain injury. It is defined by either an alteration of consciousness (feeling dazed or confused—you don't have to be knocked out) or a loss of consciousness that lasts less than 30 minutes. Being hit in the head might also cause memory loss, including loss of memories before and after the event (called *retrograde* and *anterograde* amnesia, respectively). For example, it is common for people to report that they recall being in a convoy or being on patrol before an IED explosion, but they don't remember the explosion. It is also common for them not to remember things that happened in the immediate aftermath because they are either unconscious or the blow to the head made it so they could not form new memories for a short time. Some people think that to be considered recovered, they need to regain these memories. This is not going to happen because the memories never made it into the brain for storage. In other words, it is expected that these memories will not be recovered. To be called a mild brain injury or concussion, this memory loss has to be for less than a 24-hour period. If the loss of consciousness is more than 30 minutes or the period of memory loss is greater than 24 hours, the injury is more serious than a concussion. Your medic, corpsman, or doctor will let you know whether it is a concussion as opposed to a moderate or severe brain injury.

WHAT CAN HAPPEN AFTER A CONCUSSION?

Are concussions something to worry about? Of course they are, especially right after they have occurred. As you probably already know, lots of things can happen after someone has had their bell rung. These range from mild things like confusion, which goes away pretty quickly, to things that are more serious, like a severe headache, which may take weeks to go away. Always remember that people are all different, and so not everyone will experience a concussion in the same way, but the following is a list of things that can happen.

headache	mental and physical fatigue
dizziness	lowered frustration tolerance
unsteadiness on the feet	irritability
slurred speech	apathy or poor motivation
confusion	depression
memory problems	disturbance in sleep
attention problems	nausea
slowed thinking	vomiting

Although we know a lot about concussions, what we don't know too much about is what concussive blasts do to the human brain. Obviously, blasts are important for us to know more about because many people in combat are getting concussions after an IED explodes. What we do know is that there are basically four kinds of blast effects that one might experience in the course of an explosion. The first (*primary*) is what happens to the human body because of the highly pressured blast wave itself. This is what we are learning more about because we aren't quite sure what the blast wave does to the human brain, although we know it can damage specific parts of the body. The second kind of blast effect (*secondary*) refers to when a person is thrown in the air because of the blast and then injures him- or herself because of the impact against an object or the ground. The third kind of blast effect (*tertiary*) is the damage done when other things are thrown in the air because of the force of the blast and then hit a person. The fourth (*quaternary*) effect includes other kinds of injuries related to an explosion (e.g., being burned or inhaling toxic fumes).

What's interesting with regard to concussion is that after being close to a blast, some people don't report any problems afterward and some people report physical, emotional, or cognitive symptoms.

Quick Fact

Most service members experience a full and fast recovery after a concussion.

Whether you get a concussion from a blast or a football game, however, for those who have symptoms, the good news is that they usually go away fairly quickly and there are some things you can do to make them go away as quickly as possible.

HOW DO I TAKE CARE OF MYSELF SO THAT I BEST HEAL FROM A CONCUSSION?

Healing from a concussion is mostly taken care of for you because your body and your attitude do most of the work. Just as with any other injury, the healthier you are and the better lifestyle you lead will optimize your recovery. Also, people who are better educated about concussion and who understand that full recovery from concussion is the normal course will do much better than people who are not educated and who don't think they will get better.

Here is what you can do in the few days and weeks after the concussion.

Don't Drink Alcohol

Alcohol disrupts cognitive recovery and healthy sleep cycles and makes us more likely to get hurt again.

Curb the Energy Drinks

Energy drinks have tons of caffeine and other ingredients, and we aren't really sure how some of these might affect you after a concussion.

Headaches in particular can be magnified by your body's reliance on caffeine. If you have been drinking a lot of these (more than two a day), please let your medic, corpsman, or doctor know so that they are better able to treat you (and your possible caffeine withdrawal) and understand your symptoms.

Don't Hurt Yourself Again

Seriously. After you have had a concussion you are more likely to have another one. Having had more than one makes recovery take longer. In people younger than 24, a second concussion within 4 days of the first can result in serious damage that can kill you. This sounds dramatic, but unfortunately it is the real deal. So, wear your seat belt and stay off the sports field and out of other high-risk situations until your brain is fully operational. This includes combat situations.

Take It Easy

When you still have symptoms of concussion, physical exertion only makes the symptoms worse, particularly headaches, dizziness, and visual disturbances. In fact, one of the ways we make sure your concussion symptoms are gone is to make you physically exert yourself after it looks like your symptoms are gone. If they don't come back after physical exertion, you are usually considered recovered.

Get Good Sleep

Sleeping a normal amount (not the 4-hour field amount) makes recovery go faster. If you go even one night without sleeping, consider seeing a doctor to get a sleeping medication for a couple of nights so that you can gain some control over this. People who are having problems sleeping also have problems recovering from a concussion.

Call Your Mother and Keep Your Command in the Loop

In other words, make sure you have the support that you need. People who have better social and occupational support do better after a concussion.

Know That You Will Get Better

The mind is an interesting and powerful thing. Understanding that almost everyone recovers from concussion and that you will, too, makes it more likely that not only will you recover but you also may do it more quickly than if you think you won't get better.

Follow These Recommendations

People can be finicky. You can tell them exactly the right formula for getting better, and they still think they know better than years of medical research. Do what your doctor tells you to do!

WHAT IF THE SYMPTOMS DON'T GO AWAY?

Most people recover from their concussive symptoms within a few days to a few weeks. However, it can take up to 3 months for some people's symptoms to fully resolve, and if you are reading this chapter it is possible that you fall into this category. This is normal, especially

> **Quick Fact**
>
> A healthy lifestyle and a positive attitude are the keys to recovering from a concussion.

in people who have certain risk factors (see the next section). There is a small subset of people, however, who aren't better 3 months after experiencing a concussion. We know there are some risk factors that slow down or make for an incomplete recovery. Some of these are controllable, but others are not. Let's first consider those things we can't control.

Uncontrollable Risk Factors for a Slowed Recovery

The two biggest risk factors that interfere with recovery from concussion are age and a history of prior concussions.

AGE. Younger people recover from everything faster, and concussion is no different. Older military members (senior enlisted and higher ranking officers) will take longer to recover. However, this doesn't mean that you won't recover, just that you may need to give it more time.

PRIOR CONCUSSIONS. If you've had concussions or other neurologic injury before, you might be taking longer to heal now, and the more you've had, the longer it will probably take. If this is an issue for you, it is important that you be smart when it comes to protecting your head in the future. Always wear your seat belt, motorcycle helmet, Kevlar, and so forth, and think twice before doing anything that is unnecessarily dangerous.

Quick Fact

Older people and people who have had prior concussions take longer to recover.

Controllable Risk Factors for a Slowed Recovery

There are two things you may do that can interfere with recovery from a concussion: abuse substances and fail to get help for mental health symptoms.

ALCOHOL OR DRUG ABUSE. People who abuse drugs or alcohol have worse outcomes when it comes to recovery from a concussion. We also know that if your concussion was sustained while you were drunk, you might have a harder time with recovery. Do yourself a favor, and get help if this is an issue for you. Chapter 8 of this book can help you decide whether you might have a problem and direct you to where you can get help.

MENTAL HEALTH SYMPTOMS. No one wants to hear this, but having symptoms of depression or anxiety or other problems are a very common reason why people don't feel like they are recovering from a concussion. This makes sense because many concussion symptoms are exactly the same as the symptoms for depression or PTSD. The following symptoms are exactly the same for both:

- memory problems,
- decreased frustration tolerance,
- irritability,
- decreased attention or concentration,
- fatigue or decreased energy,
- slowed thinking,
- decreased motivation,
- sleep disturbance, and
- depressed mood.

Because so many of the symptoms are the same, it can be hard for your doctor to figure out which diagnosis is causing which symptoms.

Quick Fact

If you have an alcohol problem or mental health symptoms, you might have a hard time recovering from a concussion.

The best thing to do is to get treatment for the mental health symptoms, which will likely cause the concussive symptoms to stop as well. There's one interesting thing about military members who have had a concussion and who also have mental health symptoms: Many would prefer to have symptoms caused by a concussion than by a mental health disorder. The physical injury is less stigmatizing, and many people feel that the development of mental health symptoms is a sign of weakness. No offense, but this way of thinking is a little bit nuts. Mental health symptoms are treatable! If you developed mental health symptoms in the middle of a war zone during which time someone was trying to kill you, you aren't weak, you are a patriot—go take advantage of the military medical system and get the treatment you deserve.

A FEW FINAL THOUGHTS

Concussion is a very common injury being sustained in the Iraq and Afghanistan wars because of the way the enemy fights, and a lot of people are worried about symptoms when they return from deployment. Fortunately, we know a lot about concussion because of studies with professional and collegiate athletes over the past 2 decades. The bottom line is that most people make a full recovery from a concussion or mild brain injury, and there are things you can do to optimize this recovery. Unfortunately, for a small minority of people, there are some things that can interfere with recovery: alcohol and drug abuse, mental health symptoms, older age, and a history of prior concussions. Many of these risk factors can be addressed, however, so this does not mean that people with these factors can't also get better. If you are not recovering from your concussion fully and at least 3 months have passed, you may benefit from returning to your doctor to see whether you need a referral to a neurologist or a mental health provider.

CHAPTER 14

I'M CONCERNED ABOUT MY OWN SUICIDAL THOUGHTS OR THOSE OF SOMEONE I CARE ABOUT

A lot has been lot reported lately about the increased number of suicides of service members in the Iraq and Afghanistan wars, which have gone on longer than originally expected and have resulted in more combat deployments for service members than any other war in history. This has taken its toll in many ways, one of which is the current suicide rate. Suicidal thoughts are medical emergencies that must be addressed immediately and skillfully. This chapter is for people who are having thoughts of killing or harming themselves—and for those who are worried that someone may be having these thoughts. The chapter is split into two sections: information for people who may be concerned about suicidal thoughts and information for people who have concerns about others.

Suicidal thoughts are a sign of a serious problem. Although these thoughts have many causes, what it gets right down to is that your brain chemistry isn't working correctly. If you are currently having suicidal thoughts, we urge you to get help immediately. Go to anyone in your chain of command, any mental health clinic, counseling center, or chaplain. If it is "0 dark 30" and you can't get to any of these, go to any emergency room or duty officer. All military members get suicide prevention training for a reason—go make someone use that training!

Although suicidal thinking is often temporary, it is complicated by the fact that your brain is also what is making your decisions. Think about your computer when the Internet connection isn't working right. Things usually work, but it takes forever, programs time out, things won't download, and sometimes the whole system just crashes. This is pretty similar to what is going on in your brain when suicidal thoughts start. This can result in some pretty bad thinking, and it indicates that just like your computer, you need to reboot or call in a technician.

Not to be cliché, but suicide is a permanent solution to a temporary problem. Whatever you are going through right now, even though it seems hopeless, is going to change. We know that is hard to believe because it doesn't feel like there is hope that anything can get better. But there are a lot of resources and people who can help you get it changed. You need to accept that your brain is out of whack right now, and go get help to believe and understand that your situation can change.

Service members contemplate suicide for a number of reasons. Maybe you had an unexpected or really ugly breakup. Maybe you got back from your deployment and your girlfriend or boyfriend had moved on to someone else but didn't tell you. Maybe you had something so horrible happen to you in the combat zone that you keep reliving it over and over, and think you will never be able to get

---

Quick Fact

If you are currently having suicidal thoughts, we urge you to get help immediately. There are a lot of military resources available to you if you want help.

it out of your mind. Maybe you did something in the combat zone that you aren't proud of and are questioning your right to live. Maybe your debt has gotten out of control, and you see no way out. Maybe you can't figure out where the thoughts of wanting to kill yourself started, but you have been feeling worse and worse for a long time now.

You need to understand that a decision to commit suicide has far-reaching effects. Although you may be gone, those you have left behind are not. The people who care about you very much—your parents, friends, children, significant other, and unit—will be traumatized and at risk of developing their own problems. Even though that may be hard for you to see right now, suicide is not a decision that affects only you. Your family and friends are *not* better off without you. As we said before, when you start to think about suicide, this is a serious sign that you are not thinking straight. Fortunately, there are military programs to help you with these problems and any others you might be having, and you can get access to them right now, whatever time of the day or night it happens to be.

AM I NUTS?

A lot of people with thoughts of killing themselves are concerned about what others might think, or they think that they are going crazy. And make no mistake, something is wrong with you right now—but you are definitely not nuts. You are also not weak. If you are thinking these things about yourself, you need to stop. If you are reading this chapter because you are worried about yourself, there is proof already

---

Quick Fact

If you are having thoughts of killing yourself, you aren't nuts and you aren't weak.

---

that you aren't crazy. You have recognized that your thoughts are out of whack and that you might need help.

MY CAREER WILL BE AFFECTED IF I GET HELP

No offense, but this is the least of your worries right now. If you aren't alive, your career is irrelevant. However, this is a common concern for service members with suicidal thoughts. Remember when we said earlier that your brain isn't working right? This is an example of thinking that doesn't make sense. You may have no career at all if you don't get help, and we know that people who get treatment for their thoughts go back to work when they are ready. If you get treatment, there are ways to preserve your security clearance, your flight status, or almost anything else that you are worried about.

ARE THEY GOING TO LOCK ME UP IF I TELL SOMEONE I'M HAVING SUICIDAL THOUGHTS?

Although there is a chance that you may end up on a mental health unit if you seek help for your suicidal thoughts, getting admitted to a hospital doesn't actually happen all that often, especially for someone who recognizes that there is a problem and who wants help. Most service members with thoughts of killing themselves are helped as outpatients, and for a lot of people, the thoughts go away very quickly after they have started meeting with someone and gotten help with specific problems.

Quick Fact

Most people who have career problems have them because they do not seek help.

> **Quick Fact**
>
> Your chain of command, chaplain, duty officer, mental health clinic, counseling center, and any emergency room are all ready to help you right now.

The bottom line is that you need to tell someone. Remember, go to anyone in your chain of command, any mental health clinic, counseling center, chaplain, emergency room, or duty officer.

I'M DOING OKAY, BUT I'M REALLY WORRIED ABOUT SOMEONE ELSE

As a fellow service member, you are a potential first responder, someone who is likely to be the first to know that another service member is thinking about suicide. Sometimes they will tell you on their own, but more often you will recognize the signs and risk factors and ask them yourself. The following paragraphs explain the risk factors for suicide, how to ask a service member if he or she is suicidal, what to do when he or she answers yes, and how and where to get help.

Suicide has been well studied, and a number of risk factors have been identified. No matter who you are, you should know about these. The following is a list of things to look out for or ask about. Once again, please keep in mind that everyone is different. No one

> **Quick Fact**
>
> If you are close to a service member, you are a potential first responder for suicidal thinking.

will have every risk factor on this list, and different people will have different risk factors.

- They've tried to kill themselves before.
- They have access to lethal means to kill themselves.
- They don't have a lot of social support.
- They have a drug or alcohol problem.
- They tell you they are feeling hopeless.
- They have been diagnosed with a serious mental illness.
- They have a family member who has killed him- or herself.
- They have just lost a job or a relationship or are having a financial crisis, or some other very significant stressor has occurred.

Risk factors are a little different than signs. Signs are those things that if you see them, might make it more likely that the person you care about will kill him- or herself. Again, not everyone will show the same signs, but the following signs are things to look out for.

- They are talking about death or dying.
- They have had a change in personality (e.g., becoming sad, irritable, or moody, or acting as though they don't care about anything anymore).
- They aren't interested in things they used to like, and they stop socializing.
- They have had changes in their sleep patterns (e.g., insomnia or staying in bed for much longer than usual).
- They have had changes in their eating patterns (e.g., not eating or overeating).
- They have lost interest in sex.
- They are feeling worthless, hopeless, or guilty.
- They are getting their affairs in order (e.g., revising their will, making arrangements for pets or children).

Quick Fact

Knowing the risk factors and warning signs of possible suicidal thinking can help you save a life.

- They are giving away valued possessions.
- They are drinking more or using drugs.

ASKING WHETHER SOMEONE WANTS TO KILL HIM- OR HERSELF

If after reading the preceding lists of risk factors and warning signs, you are worried, it is time to ask the question. This is a pretty uncomfortable question to ask. We worry that the people we are concerned about might be offended, that it might give them the idea of killing themselves if they haven't thought of it already, or that it might make them more likely to do it. Don't worry about these things. First, most people who are not suicidal will appreciate your concern. If they have signs and risk factors but aren't suicidal, they probably still need some help so it doesn't get that far. It's a myth that you might give them the idea to begin with or make them more likely to do it. It doesn't work that way. Suicidal thoughts are something that people come up with on their own. They aren't controllable, so don't worry about this—*just ask*.

The best way to ask is to just do it. Say, "Are you having any thoughts of killing yourself?" This makes for the most honest response

Quick Fact

Most people, when asked directly whether they are thinking of killing themselves will tell you the truth.

and makes the person give you a yes or no answer. If asked directly, most people will tell you. Vague questions such as "You aren't thinking about doing anything, are you?" don't work as well. Ask them straight and be ready for the answer.

WHAT TO DO IF THEY TELL YOU THEY ARE THINKING ABOUT SUICIDE

Don't Leave Them Alone!

If someone is thinking about suicide, don't leave him or her alone for any reason (not in the bathroom—not anywhere!). Figure out who you are going to call, and talk with the person about that. Maybe there is a specific person in the chain of command whom you think would be the best person to call. Maybe you think it should be the chaplain. Maybe you decided to call an ambulance. Whoever it is, talk it over with the service member and then make the call in front of him or her. When you've got help on the way, it's time to talk.

Talk to Them

So you got up the guts to ask and the service member told you he or she was thinking about suicide. You have found someone to help who is on the way (see the next section for more on how and where to get help). What now? Suicide is an uncomfortable topic, but what the person might need right now is someone to talk to about whatever is making him or her feel that bad. If the person wants to talk about it, let him or her, and be supportive. Let the person know that you are in this together and that you will be there for whatever he or she needs. If the person doesn't want to talk about it, shoot the sh%# about the local sports team, someone you met at a bar last weekend, or whatever you would normally talk about until the cavalry arrives.

Be There With Them Throughout the Whole Deal

If the person ends up in the emergency room, hang out with him or her until the doctors kick you out. If he or she gets admitted (which doesn't happen all that much anymore), visit when you are allowed to. If the person doesn't stay in the hospital, touch base with him or her to see how things are going. Remember, this is your friend and fellow service member, and he or she is still that same person. Go out to eat, catch a ball game, go fishing—whatever you would normally do. You don't need to mommy her or him—you just need to be there, be approachable, be understanding, and treat him or her like a normal person.

Get Rid of the Weapons and Trash the Old Prescriptions

Some service members collect firearms and knives like kids collect baseball cards. Get the weapons out of the house to a safe, secure place until the mental health provider says it is okay to give them back. Weapons should be removed immediately, and the service member should not go back into the home until they are gone. Please note that weapons are obviously personal possessions—it is best to involve the service member in the decision as to where they are going but make sure it is a place that the service member can't get access to on his or her own. If the person is not cooperative and has been deemed a risk to him- or herself, the command can trump his or her wishes about the weapons, but it is always best to avoid that whenever possible. The same goes with old pills. People tend to accumulate a lot of old prescriptions over time—trash anything that is expired and let the doctors guide you on what to do with anything that is active.

HOW AND WHERE TO GET HELP

Fortunately, the military has a lot of resources for you to get help for someone else. Where you go will depend on where you are, what time of day it is, whether the person is willing to go, and whether the person is actively trying to do something to hurt him- or herself at that moment.

Monday Through Friday During Normal Business Hours

You have the most options during this time. First, flight surgeons, primary care docs, and family medicine docs will triage someone with suicidal thoughts, and you can access these people throughout the day by calling the medical clinic. If they think the person needs help but is not in immediate danger, they may talk to the person for a while and then get him or her a routine referral to a psychology or mental health clinic. If they think the person needs help immediately, they will send him or her to the mental health clinic as an emergency walk-in. To get the person to the medical clinic, it is best to call the chain of command and let them decide whether they want to send over a senior person or a formal escort to transport or to meet you at the clinic. Depending on the situation, transportation may need to be done by ambulance (more on that in a minute). If the person is a reservist or guardsman who is not currently near his or her chain of command or any military treatment facility, the regular civilian primary care doc is the first place to go.

Any military chaplain is another option. The chaplain will likely spend time talking to the person and then help you facilitate medical evaluation. The chaplain cannot treat suicidal thinking, but chaplains are typically excellent listeners and helpers and can facilitate convincing the person to take the plunge and get formal help. Any military counseling center is another option. These counseling centers are all based on self-referrals, and you can just show up there and ask for help. Please note that just like the chaplains, these counselors cannot treat suicidal thinking; however, they can help you get where you need to go.

Calling the chain of command and letting them take over is probably the easiest way to go and ultimately the best for the service member. This allows someone else to do all of the legwork while you spend time with the person. The chain of command also has procedures already in place and will know exactly what to do and where to go. In these cases, we would recommend calling the first sergeant or other high-ranking person (the XO or deputy chief for officers) to avoid too many people in the chain of command learning about the service member's situation. However, if there is someone else whom you or the person you're helping is close to or trusts, just use your judgment about the best person to call.

After Hours

After hours, there are still many resources available. Once again, it is best to call the chain of command—this is one of the many jobs of the duty officer, and he or she will be able to guide you. You can also go to any military or civilian emergency room. If the military hospital is closest, you have to go there for reimbursement purposes if you are currently activated or are on active duty.

WHAT IF THE PERSON IS SAYING HE OR SHE IS GOING TO OR IS ACTIVELY TRYING TO HURT HIM- OR HERSELF *RIGHT NOW?*

If the person is actively suicidal and has the means to kill him- or herself where they are or you know that this is the case and are not there with them—CALL 911! At this point, you need both police intervention and emergency medical care. The service member will be transported to the hospital and will almost certainly be admitted to either a medical floor (if the person needs detoxification, e.g., or took pills or otherwise harmed him- or herself) or to the mental health unit.

A FEW FINAL THOUGHTS

Unlike some of the other things talked about in this book, suicidal thinking must be addressed by mental health professionals. It takes a lot of guts for a service member to admit that he or she is having suicidal thoughts and to ask for help. Once a person has gotten access to services, though, the situation will only get better, and service members find that relief comes relatively quickly. If you are having thoughts of suicide, go and get the help you deserve. If you are worried about someone else, help him or her get what is needed. There is help around the corner any time of day or night.

CHAPTER 15

IS IT POSSIBLE THAT I'VE CHANGED FOR THE BETTER BECAUSE OF COMBAT?

I don't know what's wrong, Doc. Ever since my truck got hit with that IED, I just don't seem myself anymore. It's hard to explain. I'm getting along with people better, and I don't get as angry as I used to. I know you're going to think I'm crazy, but sometimes it seems as if I've changed personalities with someone else. It's like the life I once knew is different and the way I look at things has changed. I don't seem to be afraid of or worry about things that I used to be afraid of or worry about. I seem to have a greater awareness of my environment and pay attention to people more. Many of the beliefs about life that I used to hold don't seem to fit with who I am. I don't even know what I believe anymore. Seriously, Doc. Am I crazy?

The answer is no. The concerns reported by the service member are not that uncommon. They are, however, difficult to describe, confusing, and sometimes troubling for the individual experiencing them. People who have experienced traumatic events make comments such as "I've changed," "I see things differently now," "People are saying I'm different, but in a good way," or "I don't feel the same anymore."

> **Quick Fact**
>
> Experiencing a traumatic event or extreme stress changes a person, and the change can be positive.

Being reminded of life and death every day and being exposed to traumatic experiences can alter how a person views the world. Not only does the way you see yourself and others change, but the rules of life change. Having your worldview turned upside down can be a hard philosophical pill to swallow, even when the change is positive.

The goals for this chapter are straightforward. First, we hope to provide you with some insight into what may be going on with you as far as this newfound change. Second, we will provide you with an explanation about what factors may have led to this change.

WHAT'S GOING ON WITH ME? A CHANGE FOR THE BETTER

Alfred Adler, a well-known Austrian physician and psychologist, believed that an individual's personality could be changed by experiencing a traumatic event. Events such as rape, providing medical care to a badly injured friend on the battlefield, or narrowly escaping death or injury from an IED blast can jolt a person's psyche to the point that his or her view of the world, self, and others is turned upside down. Specifically, the experience causes the person to challenge his or her previously held beliefs.

> **Quick Fact**
>
> An individual's personality changes after being exposed to a traumatic event.

More contemporary views of the change that occurs after trauma have developed over recent years. Posttraumatic growth (PTG) is a concept that is currently receiving much attention in the psychological and psychiatric communities, particularly with veterans. PTG is a scientific and philosophical approach to understanding the positive changes that can occur in individuals after being exposed to a traumatic experience. In the past, trauma has been viewed as a cause of psychological dysfunction. However, the research has shown that many people don't develop chronic problems. Furthermore, for quite some time, experts have been aware that some individuals actually become emotionally and socially healthier after exposure to trauma. Take the example of Staff Sergeant B.

Staff Sergeant B. is an 11-year veteran of the U.S. Army. Over the past several years, he has deployed five times to Iraq in support of Operation Iraqi Freedom. As a career infantryman, he has always prided himself in his strong commitment to the army, his expert skills as an infantryman, and the respect he has earned from those under him. However, the multiple deployments, a recent divorce from his wife of 12 years, and long-standing anger and resentment toward his father, who has recently been diagnosed with lung cancer, are taking a tremendous toll on him. As might be expected, his view of life has become more negative and cynical. There have even been periods when he has contemplated suicide. Fortunately, a strong relationship with his unit chaplain has gotten him through these difficult times.

Three weeks before his redeployment, Staff Sergeant B.'s Humvee was struck with a roadside IED while out on patrol. Although his team survived the initial blast, two of his soldiers were killed, and he was severely injured when a secondary IED detonated as they were dismounting the truck and searching the area for insurgents. After a 4-week stay at a regional medical center and a near full recovery, Staff Sergeant B. was sent home to be with his unit.

During a routine interview with one of the base psychologists, Staff Sergeant B. reported difficulty falling asleep, occasional nightmares, distressing flashbacks of the event, and grief about the deaths of his men. However, to the surprise of the psychologist, Staff Sergeant B.'s views about life were changing and becoming more positive and optimistic. Just in the short time at home, he made amends to his ex-wife and apologized for his behaviors that contributed to the divorce. He also visited his dying father in the hospital and subsequently spent the next 3 months by his side repairing the relationship. Over the next several months, Staff Sergeant B. has become involved with various volunteer organizations in his community, and those who know him best comment on how much he has changed and what a pleasant and inspirational person he is to be around.

The story of Staff Sergeant B. is one that military mental health professionals are hearing often. Instead of being disabled by the traumatic experiences that are common on the battlefield, service members are growing psychologically, spiritually, and emotionally. Fortunately, our knowledge in this area is growing as well, which will lead to a better level of care and better outcomes for service members returning from combat.

FACTORS THAT MAY CONTRIBUTE TO THE CHANGE

Now that you are aware that some people change in a positive direction after exposure to trauma, let's talk about factors that may be involved in this growth. Some experts equate PTG with a sort of psychological earthquake. Just as a building's foundation can shift after an earthquake, how a person views and interprets the world can be shaken by a traumatic event or series of traumatic events. Previously held beliefs are replaced by more adaptive or consistent ones that fit with the traumatic experience. For example, after narrowly escaping serious injury or death, a service member may develop a greater

> **Quick Fact**
>
> Our strongly held, lifelong beliefs can change after a traumatic event.

appreciation for life by incorporating a core belief such as "Life is precious, and I should be thankful for each day I have on Earth." A service member who loses a best friend to a Humvee rollover accident develops a new belief, such as "Loved ones can leave this world at any moment. It's important to spend as much time with them as you can." These new beliefs can shape many aspects of a person's life. Remember, thoughts have a significant impact on how people feel and behave.

The concept of psychological resiliency, or being able to bounce back from adversity, has often been discussed alongside PTG. Researchers, particularly those working with veterans, are currently studying the characteristics shared by individuals who show signs of psychological resiliency. To date, some factors associated with this enhanced psychological resiliency include flexibility, a tendency to be optimistic, using humor as a form of coping, having supportive friends and family members, and an internal locus of control (i.e., believing one has control over the events in one's lives). It is quite possible that those who have greater psychological resiliency have a greater chance of experiencing PTG. The good news is that we know psychological resiliency can be taught and learned. Predeployment programs for service members are now underway that focus on education about stress and resiliency, increasing coping skills, promoting healthy lifestyles, and effective ways to take care of yourself and your battle buddy.

As you can see, a number of factors likely contribute to creating positive meaning and change when one is faced with adversity.

> **Quick Fact**
>
> Psychological resiliency can be learned.

It is not as simple as being positive or thinking good thoughts but a combination of preexisting personality traits, childhood experiences, social supports, and cultural influences. So, thinking back to high school science, it appears to be a combination of nature and nurture.

A FEW FINAL THOUGHTS

Humans have been trying to understand the meaning of suffering since the beginning of humankind. However, it has only been in the past 50 years or so that scientists have really attempted to study the phenomenon of positive change that occurs after trauma. The shift between looking at trauma through the lens of growth rather than dysfunction is a welcome and timely one.

It is important for you to realize that even when a person experiences positive growth from a traumatic experience, significant emotional and psychological pain often accompanies that growth. As a result, it is important to allow yourself to deal with the pain surrounding the trauma and not force yourself in a direction that your mind and body may not be ready to take you. Remember, slow can be fast.

For those of you who have experienced traumatic events on the battlefield, life does not have to be a constant struggle from here on out. We are learning more and more each day about how the human mind works. As mentioned earlier, more effective treatments for disorders like posttraumatic stress disorder are being developed, and predeployment training for service members that focuses on building psychological resiliency is being implemented. Your service and sacrifices have far-reaching effects.

Finally, if you are able to find some time in your busy schedule, maybe during your postdeployment leave, we recommend you read the book *Man's Search for Meaning* by Victor Frankl. Frankl provides a very profound and influential personal essay about his imprisonment in several Nazi concentration camps over a number of years and his struggle during this time to find meaning in life, particularly a reason to live. His story—and his life—is truly one of overcoming adversity and the reality of positive growth after trauma.

APPENDIX: RESOURCES FOR YOU AND YOUR FAMILY

Deployments are tough on both the service member and his or her family. The good news is that you are not alone. There are hundreds of resources, organizations, and programs currently available that provide valuable information and countless services and benefits to service members and their families. Some organizations are sponsored by governmental agencies, and others are run by volunteers and kept afloat by private donations.

In this Appendix, we provide information on a small sample of resources and the larger group of organizations across this country dedicated to helping service members and their families. Again, this is not a comprehensive list, and there are countless other resources and organizations out there that provide great services to service members and their families. Our not including them here is merely a consequence of limited space.

One last note: The contact information for the following organizations and programs was up to date at the time of this writing. As you well know, things change. If a URL or phone number is no longer valid for a particular site, keep trying. Please also note that some of these organizations perform multiple functions.

RESOURCES FOR CHILDREN

Please note that there are now many books for children about military deployments. Many of these may be found in your local library, and all may be found on any book-selling website. The following list is just a sample.

- *Daddy's in Iraq, But I Want Him Back* by Carmen R. Hoyt, published by Trafford (2005)
- *I Miss You! A Military Kid's Book About Deployment* by Beth Andrews and Hawley Wright, published by Prometheus Books (2007)
- *My Dad's a Hero* by Rebecca Christiansen and Jewel Armstrong, published by Word Association (2007)
- *My Mommy Wears Combat Boots* by Sharon McBride, published by AuthorHouse (2008)
- *When Dad's at Sea* by Mindy L. Pelton, published by Albert Whitman (2004)
- *Deployment Journal for Kids* by Rachel Robertson, published by Elva Resa (2005)
- *Flat Daddies and Flat Mommies* (http://flatdaddies.com/): Families can order free of charge a life-sized poster of a deployed mom or dad for military children.
- *Sesame Street's Sesame Workshop* (http://www.sesamework shop.org/initiatives/emotion/tlc): Provides several videos for kids about deployments and homecoming.

RESOURCES FOR FAMILIES

Please note that many of the resources listed for service members here also include resources for families. If you don't find something that you are looking for here, try the next section.

- *Air Force Crossroads* (http://www.afcrossroads.com): Air Force Crossroads is the U.S. Air Force community website that provides information to airmen and their families on topics such as parenting, relocation, education, employment, finances, deployment, and postdeployment. It also includes a forum for airmen to give advice and receive advice from other airmen.
- *American Veterans With Brain Injuries* (http://www.avbi.org): American Veterans With Brain Injuries is a not-for-profit organization that provides support to veterans and their families.
- *Coming Home Project* (http://www.cominghomeproject.net): The Coming Home Project is a nonprofit organization devoted to providing care and support to Iraq and Afghanistan veterans and their families. The organization assists military members and their families with emotional, spiritual, and relationship problems before, during, and after deployment.
- *Fallen Patriot Fund* (http://www.fallenpatriotfund.org): The Fallen Patriot Fund helps families of U.S. military personnel who were killed or seriously injured during Operation Iraqi Freedom. Support to the families is primarily financial in nature.
- Family services and individual service member support: These organizations provide a wide variety of services to service members and their families, including individual and marital therapy, financial counseling, and many other support services—Air Force Family Support (http://www.afcrossroads.com), Army Community Services (http://www.myarmylifetoo.com), Marine Corps Community Services (http://www.usmc-mccs.org/), National Guard Bureau State Family Programs (http://www.guardfamily.org and http://www.guardfamilyyouth.org), and Navy Fleet and Family Support (http://www.ffsp.navy.mil/ or http://www.lifelines.navy.mil).
- *Fisher House* (http://www.fisherhouse.org): Fisher House provides lodging and support to military family members so

that families can be close to their loved ones during times of hospitalization.

- *Gold Star Family* (http://www.goldstarfamilysupportgroup.com/): Gold Star Family provides programs and support to address the needs of families who have lost a service member.
- *Military Impacted Schools Association* (http://www.militarystudent.org): This organization supports schools with high concentrations of military children. In addition, it provides resources related to frequent transitions and resilience for children during parental deployment.
- *Military Money* (http://www.militarymoney.com): Military Money provides information about finances for military families to ensure military readiness of the service member and financial stability of the family.
- *Military OneSource* (http://militaryonesource.com; 1-800-342-9647): Military OneSource is a one-stop organization for service members and their families dealing with any type of problem. From child care to getting help paying the electric bill, Military OneSource is available 24 hours a day, 365 days a year. One unique benefit Military OneSource provides is referral for free (up to several sessions) mental health evaluation and counseling for veterans and active service members.
- *National Military Family Association* (http://www.nmfa.org): The National Military Family Association provides wide-ranging family support services and programs for military families. One of the more popular programs is the Operation Purple Summer Camps for children.
- *Operation Military Kids* (http://www.operationmilitarykids.org): This organization provides a wide range of information on access resources for military children.
- *TRICARE* (http://www.tricare.mil): TRICARE is the health care program serving active duty, National Guard, and Reserve

military members, retirees, their families, survivors, and certain former spouses worldwide. TRICARE brings together health care resources of the uniformed services and supplements them with networks of civilian health care professionals, institutions, pharmacies and suppliers to provide access to high-quality health care services while maintaining the capability to support military operations.

- *Your Soldier, Your Army: A Parent's Guide* (http://www3.ausa. org/webpub/deptfamilyprograms.nsf/byid/kcat-6hch3x): This is a book (free online) for concerned parents of young service members.

RESOURCES FOR SERVICE MEMBERS

- *On Combat: The Psychology and Physiology of Deadly Conflict in War and in Peace* by Dave Grossman and Loren W. Christensen, published by Warrior Science (2008)
- *On Killing: The Psychological Cost of Learning to Kill in War and Society* by Dave Grossman, published by Little, Brown (1996)
- *After Deployment* (http://www.afterdeployment.org): After Deployment is a psychological wellness website that assists service members, veterans, and families with managing after-deployment problems or concerns. Not only does it include resources for obtaining psychological help, it provides psychological self-assessment tools and stories from other service members and veterans.
- *BATTLEMIND* (http://www.battlemind.army.mil/): BATTLE-MIND is a multimedia program that assists with orienting the service member to the predeployment and postdeployment cycles. It also provides training for spouses, children, and military leaders.

- *Center for Women Veterans* (http://www1.va.gov/womenvet/):
  The Center for Women Veterans is a branch of the Department
  of Veterans Affairs (VA) tasked with ensuring that the needs
  of female veterans are met. It provides a number of links to
  services for women.
- *Defense Finance Accounting Service (DFAS) MyPay* (https://
  mypay.dfas.mil/mypay.aspx): DFAS can provide assistance when
  a service member is having pay or benefits problems.
- *Defense and Veterans Brain Injury Center* (http://dvbic.org):
  DVBIC serves service members, family members, and veterans
  who have brain injuries.
- *Department of Defense Sexual Assault Prevention and Response*
  (http://www.sapr.mil): This website provides information on
  military sexual assault policies and training and resources for
  people who need help and the different types of reporting options.
- *Disabled American Veterans* (http://www.dav.org): The Disabled American Veterans program provides support to disabled
  veterans and their families. This is a great source for information on how the Veterans Affairs disability and compensation
  system works.
- *Employer Support of the Guard and Reserve* (http://www.
  esgr.org): Employer Support of the Guard and Reserve is a
  Department of Defense program that assists Guard and Reserve
  members of the military with resolving employee–employer conflicts related to military service through mediation and education.

FINANCIAL MANAGEMENT

- Checking your credit report: http://www.annualcreditreport.com
- Homeowner assistance for members of the Armed Forces
  permanently reassigned during specified mortgage crisis: http://
  www.sas.usace.army.mil/hapinv/index.html

- Military handbooks addressing a variety of issues, including pay, medical, college, and retirement benefits: http://www.military handbooks.com/
- *Military Money Magazine:* http://www.militarymoney.com
- *Military One Source:* This general website can address pretty much any question related to any personal issue for service members: http://www.militaryonesource.com
- National Guard money matters and a variety of other state-specific services: http://www.guardfamily.org
- *Office of the Secretary of Defense Military Compensation website:* Provides information about military pay and allowances, retirement, Thrift Savings Plan, benefits and survivor benefits. Includes pay and allowance and retirement calculations. http://militarypay.defense.gov/
- Service-specific financial resources: U.S. Air Force, http://www.afcrossroads.com; U.S. Army, http://www.myarmylifetoo.com; Marine Corps, http://www.usmc-mccs.org/finance/index.cfm; and U.S. Navy, http://www.nffsp.org
- *Fund for Veterans' Education* (http://www.veteransfund.org): The Fund for Veterans' Education provides scholarships to veterans from all branches of the military who served in Afghanistan or Iraq since September 11, 2001, and who are now enrolled in college or vocational–technical school.
- *Hooah 4 Health* (http://www.hooah4health.com/): This is an army program geared to address health in four dimensions: body, mind, spirit, and environment. Also includes resources for spouses and children.
- *Military.com's Military Benefits site* (http://www.military benefits.com): A comprehensive website dedicated to the wide variety of benefits available to active, Reserve, and Guard members.

- *Military Pathways* (http://www.militarymentalhealth.org): Military Pathways is a Department of Defense program that offers mental health self-assessment and referral services to military members and their families through taking anonymous mental health and alcohol use assessments online, via phone, and through special events held at military installations.
- *Military Service Relief Societies:* These organizations provide emergency financial assistance, budget counseling, and scholarships: Air Force Aid Society (http://www.afas.org), Army Emergency Relief (http://www.aerhq.org), Navy–Marine Corps Relief Society (http://www.nmcrs.org), National Guard OnLine Community (http://www.guardfamily.org).
- *My GI Bill* (http://www.mygibill.org): My GI Bill provides up-to-date information on the military's GI Bill and information about the Post-9/11 Veterans Educational Assistance Act of 2008.
- *National Amputation Foundation* (http://www.national amputation.org): This group provides assistance to veterans of any war with an amputation.
- *National Center for PTSD* (http://www.ncptsd.va.gov): The National Center for PTSD is a VA program that advances the mental health care of veterans through research, education, and training. There are numerous resources on the center's website about posttraumatic stress disorder and veterans.
- *National Suicide Prevention Lifeline* (1-800-273-8255): The National Suicide Prevention Lifeline is a toll-free, 24-hour suicide crisis line. Tell the operator that you are a veteran, and you will be put in touch with someone who can help you. All calls are confidential.
- *National Veterans Foundation* (http://www.nvf.org): The National Veterans Foundation provides "crisis management, information and referral needs of all U.S. Veterans and their families" (http://www.nvf.org/pages/mission). Outreach services

include assistance with food, clothing, transportation, employment, and other relevant services to military members.

- *National Veterans Legal Services Program* (http://www.nvlsp. org): The National Veterans Legal Services Program provides free legal assistance to veterans and service members of Operation Iraqi Freedom and Operation Enduring Freedom.
- *Substance abuse and gambling:* These websites provide information about substance abuse and gambling problems and include how to find a meeting wherever you are: Alcoholics Anonymous, http://www.aa.org; Gamblers Anonymous, http://www.gambler sanonymous.org; and Narcotics Anonymous, http://www.na.org.
- *U.S. Department of Veterans Affairs* (http://www.va.gov): The VA's mission is to provide excellence in patient care, veterans benefits, and customer satisfaction. The VA handles issues such as the GI Bill, disability, pension and compensation, and health care for veterans.
- *Warrior Care* (http://www.warriorcare.mil): Warrior Care is a Department of Defense portal that includes links to various health-related programs for the U.S. Army, Navy, Air Force, and Marine Corps. It provides links to services for active duty, Reserve, and National Guard military members and their families.
- *Women's Trauma Recovery Program* (http://www.womenvets PTSD.va.gov): This is a residential program for female veterans with PTSD related to military service. Most of the women treated here have experienced military sexual trauma. This program is open to women across the country.

RESOURCES FOR MENTAL HEALTH PROVIDERS

Please note that all of the resources listed in this Appendix are also excellent resources for providers, for both your own education and being able to help your clients access other services. The following are just a few of our own most-often used references.

Freeman, S. M., Moore, B. A., & Freeman, A. (2009). *Living and surviving in harm's way: A psychological treatment handbook for pre- and post-deployment of military personnel.* New York, NY: Routledge.

Hall, L. K. (2008). *Counseling military families: What mental health providers need to know.* New York, NY: Routledge.

Kennedy, C. H., & Zillmer, E. A. (2006). *Military psychology: Clinical and operational applications.* New York, NY: Guilford Press.

Moore, B. A., & Jongsma, A. (2009). *The veterans and active duty military psychotherapy treatment planner.* New York, NY: Wiley.

INDEX

AA. *See* Alcoholics Anonymous
Acceptance, of killing, 107
Acknowledgment
  of anger, 24
  of children's behavior, 66, 67
  of shame and guilt of killing, 111
Acting out
  as defense mechanism, 108
  by school-age children, 63, 67
Active-duty service members, 4, 39
Actively suicidal people, 151–152
Activity(-ies)
  in bed, 34
  and grief, 101
Addiction, 85–95
  and alcohol use, 86–87
  and career, 92–93
  confronting others about, 93–94
  and coping, 94–95
  and drug use, 88–89
  and gambling, 89–90
  treatment for, 90–93
Adler, Alfred, 154
Adultery, 55
Adversity, 157, 159
Afghanistan war, 139, 141. *See also*
  Operation Enduring Freedom
After Deployment (website), 165

Age, 61, 137
Aggression, in preschoolers, 63
Air Force Aid Society, 168
Air Force Crossroads, 163
Air Force Family Support, 163
Alcoholics Anonymous (AA), 91, 169
Alcohol use, 86–87
  and anger, 23
  confronting others about, 93–94
  and grief, 97, 102
  in postdeployment period, 13, 16
  and recovery from concussions, 134,
    138
  and relaxation, 120
  resources for support, 168
  as self-medicating, 94–95
  treatment for, 90–92
American Veterans With Brain Injuries,
  163
Amnesia, 132
Amputation assistance, 168
Anger, 19–28
  causes of, 21–22
  controlling, 24–28
  and grief, 97–98
  negative and positive impact of, 19,
    22–24
  of school-age children, 64

ABOUT THE AUTHORS

Bret A. Moore, PsyD, ABPP, is a former active-duty U.S. Army psychologist and two-tour veteran of Operation Iraqi Freedom. During his 27 months deployed to Iraq, he provided counseling to thousands of service members for problems such as depression, anger, and posttraumatic stress disorder. He is the author and editor of three other books: *Living and Surviving in Harm's Way, The Veterans and Active Duty Military Psychotherapy Treatment Planner,* and *Pharmacotherapy for Psychologists.* Dr. Moore also writes a biweekly column titled *Kevlar for the Mind,* which is published in *Army Times, Air Force Times, Navy Times,* and *Marine Corps Times.* His views and opinions on military psychology have been quoted in *USA Today, The New York Times, The Boston Globe,* NPR, BBC, and CBC. Dr. Moore writes a regular blog on mental health topics for service members and their families. It can be found at www.psychologytoday.com/blog/the-camouflage-couch.

Carrie H. Kennedy, PhD, ABPP, is a lieutenant commander in the Medical Service Corps of the U.S. Navy. She currently serves as an aerospace psychologist at the Naval Aerospace Medical Institute. Dr. Kennedy is the U.S. Navy's only dual-designated clinical and aerospace experimental psychologist. She serves as the chair of the Conflict of Interest Committee for the National Academy of Neuropsychology, is the past chair of the American Psychological Association's Division 19 (Military Psychology) Ethics Consultation Committee, and serves as member-at-large of Division 19. She is the coeditor of *Military Psychology: Clinical and Operational Applications* and *Military Neuropsychology.* She serves on the editorial boards of *Military Psychology* and *Psychological Services.*